Because
I Said So

SHARI LOW has published twenty novels over
the last two decades. She also writes for newspapers,
magazines and television. Once upon a time, she got
engaged to a guy she'd known for a week, and twenty-
something years later, they live in Glasgow with their
two teenage sons and a labradoodle.

Because I Said So

SHARI LOW

HEAD
ZEUS

An Anima Book

This is an Anima book, first published in the UK
in 2018 by Head of Zeus Ltd

9 7 5 3 1 2 4 6 8

A catalogue record for this book is available from
the British Library.

ISBN (HB): 9781786696731
ISBN (E): 9781786696724

Typeset by Adrian McLaughlin

Printed and bound in Great Britain by
CPI Group (UK) Ltd, Croydon CR0 4YY

Head of Zeus Ltd
First Floor East
5–8 Hardwick Street
London EC1R 4RG
WWW.HEADOFZEUS.COM

To the Low guys, John, Callan and Brad, for giving me endless
disasters, dramas and laughs to write about.
I love you all more than words...
Now can someone go put the washing machine on.

How it began...

Back in 2004, when my sons, Callan and Brad, were one and three, I began writing a weekly column documenting the ups, down, and hazardous laundry baskets of family life. Now those little chicks are teenagers who are fleeing the nest, leaving behind a mother with soggy feathers (no, I wasn't weeping tears of woe, there was something in my eye) and a collection of tales about getting it right, getting it wrong, mortifying mistakes, disastrous summer holidays, childhood milestones, Christmas catastrophes, things that made me laugh and, in the case of nativity plays and eight bouts of chickenpox, the things that made me cry.

These are my favourite stories, spanning pregnancy, babyhood, toddlerdom, school years (when I changed their names to Low The Elder and Low The Younger to protect their privacy), and now the bit when they leave home and I adopt a veneer of stoic encouragement while wondering what to do with the empty room, the extra free time and the cash saved on the weekly food bill.

Because I Said So

Whether you're pregnant for the first time, or already have a brood of adult children, I hope you'll find something here that will make you smile and nod in recognition.

And boys, if you're reading this, don't hold any of the mishaps against me. We made it to adulthood and you're still talking to me. You turned out great. I'd do it all again. And you'll be fine as long as you remember the lessons I taught you...

Your mother is allowed to be embarrassing.

Everyone has cute childhood memories that make them blush. Although most of yours do involve pants.

And, obviously, your mamma is always right... *because I said so.* ◆

2004

Toddler Spots and Burnt Pots ››››

Just Call Me Flo...

If I were on the nightshift in the medical tent during the Crimean War, history would read very differently. Instead of Florence Nightingale, the Lady of the Lamp, it would be Shari Low, lady of the dodgy diagnostic skills, who trotted up and down the ranks, bellowing, 'Look, if you don't stop that moaning you're getting nothing for your tea.'

There's as much chance of me winning a Carer of the Year award as there is of Victoria Beckham popping into Primark for her spring/summer wardrobe.

On Monday, I noticed a large spot on Callan's head. Now, at three, he's ten years too young for puberty so I was a wee bit concerned. I showed it to assorted family members. Opinion was split between, 'och, it's just a plook,' and long inhalations through pursed lips, accompanied by, 'it looks like chickenpox.'

Absolutely not! Callan has already had chickenpox twice so I knew it couldn't be that.

However, by next morning he looked like one of those cartoons, where a small child doesn't want to go to school so he draws hundreds of spots all over his face and body with red felt-tip. The horror of it was that I knew Cal didn't have a red felt-tip (confiscated after Bob the Builder, Scoop and Dizzy were drawn on our freshly painted bedroom wall).

I screamed for the husband. 'What do you think?' I gasped in an anguished screech that suitably reflected my usual tendency towards the overdramatic. I was already imagining wild, exotic infections (ignoring the fact that the furthest afield we've been in the last year is Penrith) that would require at least six months of quarantine for the whole family.

'Chickenpox?' he replied with a shrug.

'Absolutely not, he's already had it twice,' I said fretfully.

I whisked Callan up – at arm's length – to the doctors' surgery, where the spotty wee soul was thoroughly examined.

'Chickenpox' was the diagnosis.

'But it can't be, he's already had it twice,' I protested yet again, before running him through every other possibility I could think of. There was I, every shred of medical knowledge I possessed gained from watching *ER* and *Casualty*, and I was arguing with a man of thirty years' experience in general practice.

'My dear, this is definitely chickenpox,' he replied dryly, as he scribbled a note on Cal's file – probably along the lines of 'Mother is argumentative, neurotic and please put her on that special list of people we're trying to bump to another practice.'

So there it was. Chickenpox.

Now, being fully aware that I was behind a steel-plated, time-alarmed, impenetrable door when God gave out the 'empathy and sympathy for itchy ailments' genes, I made a very special effort to summon my nursing skills.

For the first twenty-four hours I was a model of care and concern. I cuddled him close when he cried because his friends couldn't come to play. I patiently mashed up fruit when he couldn't swallow anything hard because the spots were in his throat. I got up every few hours during the night to dab calamine lotion on his skin. I even slept in his arthritis-inducing-if-you're-over-the-age-of-eight bed all night so that I was near him on the 106 occasions that he woke up moaning about the discomfort.

On day two I cracked.

My faulty genes and chronic sleep deprivation kicked in and I realised that I couldn't do another day of soothing words, gentle rubs and reading *How Much Do I Love You* on a repetitive loop.

I dispatched the husband to the shops for emergency rations: ten bags of chocolate buttons, *Monsters Inc.*, *Toy Story 2*, *Shrek*, and a balaclava so that I could take Cal for walks without scaring the neighbours.

And so we established McSpotty's daily pattern for the rest of the week: unlimited bribery with chocolate, more television than the average couch potato gets through in a month, and a nightly walk with him dressed like an armed robber.

Medical input from mummy? Limited to regular hugs, sympathetic smiles and a wee rub of the head every time I passed him en route to change the video.

Last night in bed, inspired by our current situation, I told Cal the story of Florence Nightingale, explaining what a gentle and kind nurse she was, how she instinctively knew what was wrong with the sick and how best to comfort them.

He pondered this for a few moments.

Eventually, he spoke.

'Mummy, you're a rubbish nurse.'

It's the best diagnosis that's been made in this house all week. ◆

To the Infirmary and Beyond

According to my son, his name isn't Callan Low. It's Lightyear. Buzz Lightyear, Space Commander, sworn enemy of the evil Emperor Zurg. We just call him Buzz for short.

From the minute the three-year-old with the vivid imagination first encountered Mr Lightyear, he's been saving the planet on a daily basis. Since this invariably involves jumping from a great height shouting 'To infinity and beyond', the rest of the family live in a state of constant fear – husband and I are terrified that he'll hurt himself, while Brad (nearly two) is terrified that his superhero brother will land on him.

We've had many near tragedies since Callan became Buzz. He recently leapt from the top of a flight of stairs, accompanied by the mandatory yell of, 'To infinity and beeeeeeeeeee…' That was as far as he got before he landed halfway down and, by some miracle, survived with only a bruised bottom to show for the adventure.

A few days later, he jumped into a swimming pool, uttering the same war cry. He neglected to notice that Buzz doesn't come complete with armbands and a dinghy, and we had to fish him out before he sank like an intergalactic stone.

But a couple of nights ago we had our biggest adventure yet. We thought our home was relatively Buzz-safe – locked doors, reinforced furniture, bouncy carpets. However, we neglected to remove a lethal weapon from the bathroom: the towel rail. Apparently, the universe was in jeopardy again and the only thing that could save it was Buzz swinging on the towel rail, before doing a triple-back summersault and ending up sprawled on the bathroom floor. Did I mention that his head struck the metal toilet roll holder on the way down? Bog roll one, Buzz Lightyear nil.

The screams had us galloping to the bathroom and I nearly fainted at the sight. There was so much blood it looked like he'd ruptured a main artery. I turned him around to see a crater the size of a small planet on the back of his skull. Actually it was a gash about an inch long, but I was in drama/panic mode and convinced he had only minutes to live.

We bundled a bemused Brad and a hysterical Buzz into the car and raced to the hospital.

'To the infirmary and beyond...'

Naturally, by the time we got there, Buzz was completely back to normal and, other than the red stuff oozing from his skull, looked like he didn't have a care in the world. Apparently, space commanders have supernatural powers of recovery. Meanwhile, my heart was still thumping like a hut door in a hurricane and the fright had put me into such a state of hypertension that I sounded like I'd been sniffing helium.

The hospital checked us in and directed us to wait in the seated area. Two hours later, it was me who was climbing the walls. Not because I was still panicking over the health of my firstborn, but because he'd made such a rapid recovery that he was chasing his wee brother (now renamed The Evil Emperor Zurg) around the room and was in danger of causing yet another injury. By the time the doctor called us in, all shreds of sympathy had vanished and I was ready to ground Buzz for the rest of his life.

The doc examined his wound carefully. And can I just point out at this stage that not all ER doctors look like George Clooney. Not that I minded, because I had hair like a burst couch, no make-up on, was dressed in my pyjamas and covered in blood. But we definitely didn't get George. We got that bloke from Hellraiser.

'Needs a few stitches,' he declared. No problem, I thought. A few stitches are nothing to a superhero. Then I saw the doc loading the local aesthetic into a syringe that was so huge it looked like it was designed for horses. Buzz saw it too. Who knew action figures could retreat so quickly?

The doctor administered several jabs to the back of the head, while I tried my best to utter soothing words. As the needle went in, I did what I always do when the kids are scared, upset or sleepy – I decided to sing a song. Only my mind was blank. I couldn't think of a single lyric except… 'Jingle Bells'. Picture the scene. An impatient doctor trying to administer an anaesthetic to a wriggling child, while a demented mother with tears blinding her, clutches on to her son's ears and sings 'Jingle Bells' at the top of her voice. In the middle of March.

I tried to reassure my boy. 'Almost done, baby, almost done, you're such a brave boy, oh what fun it is to ride in a one horse open sleigh…'

Almost done? I could have run up a new set of curtains in the time it took Hellraiser to insert three stitches in my frenzied superhero's head.

Finally it was finished, and the doctor gladly fled the scene, leaving the lovely nurse to dress the wound. She wrapped a bandage around my warrior's head and the minute I saw it my stomach sank. Buzz Lightyear was gone, but in his place we had Rambo.

Thankfully, he didn't need further treatment; although we are avoiding the local parks for fear that he'll indulge in a spot of jungle warfare or attempt to take a parkie hostage.

However, my recovery from the trauma has been slower and required a repeat prescription for a large bottle of plonk.

'To oblivion and beyond…' ◆

Trick or Treat?

'Mummy, I'm going to be a PUMP...' my three-year-old, Callan, announced at full volume in the middle of the local library last week.

I clenched my eyes shut tight in trepidation as to the inevitable infant-logic explanation that would follow. As regular readers know, Cal has an affinity for the word 'pump', usually applied at the most inappropriate times (i.e. meeting elderly aunties at family functions – 'How are you, Callan?' 'Pump' is the reply).

'Pardon?' I replied with as much nonchalance as I could muster, hoping that his toddler attention span had already moved on to what he wanted for his tea.

'I'm going to be a PUMP... KIN,' he proclaimed proudly.

'Me too,' piped up his two-year-old brother, Brad. Of course, Brad has no idea what he's talking about, but just as Callan loves the word 'pump', Brad (aka, The Echo) automatically adds 'Me too' to the end of all his brother's sentences. If Cal announced that when he grows up he's going to be a classical pianist, change his name to Farquhar and adopt a diet of nothing but mushrooms, Brad would pipe up with the obligatory, 'Me too'.

But back to the library.

'When?' I asked, mystified.

'At the Halloween party.'

Oh, groan. Halloween. The day of the year that I dread even more than Valentine's Day, my wedding anniversary and National No Moaning Day. It's bad enough that I get forty-seven kids at the door, in various plastic masks demanding fun-size Mars bars and fifty pence for telling a joke about a chicken and a cow. But since my boys are only two and three, I thought I had a few years left yet before I had to start dealing with the pressures of costume planning and freezing my bits off as I traipse around the neighbourhood accompanied by a headless horseman and Donald Duck.

But apparently Callan had other ideas. It turns out that, not only is there a fancy dress party in his nursery tomorrow, but his friends have also filled his head with the joyous rewards of venturing out on Halloween.

It's one of those defining tests of motherhood, isn't it?

Surely, if I were a dedicated, creative earth mother, then I would spend hours with my sewing machine, running up a costume masterpiece that could be forever preserved in in a glass display case at the Museum of Modern Art. Or perhaps I'd take the consumer route and blow a weekly wage on an authentic Goofy suit.

Trick or Treat?

Does the fact that I'm tempted to cut a sheet in half, rip holes in the middle and tell them that they're ghosts make me a maternal washout?

I decided to tackle the problem head on. If they had to do the whole dressing up thing, then pumpkins were out of the question – I don't have anything remotely pumpkin-like that can be adapted to outerwear for infants. The only thing in our house that's round and orange is my face after a dodgy fake-tan session.

'Is there anything else you'd like to dress up as?' I asked hopefully.

'A Power Ranger,' was the enthusiastic answer.

'Me too,' agreed The Echo.

Damn. I don't keep a stock of fluorescent jumpsuits and crash helmets in primary colours.

'Anything else?'

'Batman,' was the next suggestion.

'Me too,' said The Echo.

Nope, last time I checked I didn't have a stockpile of black balaclavas, capes or 100-denier tights.

I was getting desperate.

'Anything else?'

His wee face lit up in a flash of inspiration.

'I could be a mummy!' he announced triumphantly.

'Me too.'

At last we were getting somewhere. I was sure I had a box of crepe bandages lurking in the cupboard of miscellaneous plasters, cotton buds and out-of-date bottles of Tixylix that masquerades as our first aid kit. Granted they're ones left over from husband's footballing injuries, so they're a bit worn around the edges and stink of vapour rub, but they'd do.

'Great idea,' I congratulated him. 'You'd be just like the scary mummy in *Scooby Doo*.'

'No, not that kind of mummy. A real mummy. With a baby and a pram.'

'Me too.'

My heart sank. We're all for dispelling gender stereotypes, but I was all out of small 'mummy' clothes, all out of babies, and all out of prams.

It took some deft negotiation, but we eventually came to an agreement. So on Sunday night, if you open the door to two wee ghosts and a deranged-looking blonde, be generous with the Mars bars. It'll be worth it. I know a great joke about a chicken and a cow. ◆

The Ambush

Newsflash – I've decided that those so-called 'superwomen' who claim that they can easily combine motherhood with a career are lying through their teeth. I seem to permanently tread a middle ground somewhere between calamity and chaos.

On Friday, I had an early morning meeting scheduled with a big-shot Hollywood agent to discuss plans to get my new novel adapted for film or television. It sounds very glam, but honestly it's not. I had the same meeting after I'd finished my previous three books and none of them ever made it to the silver screen. It'll all go pear-shaped and I'll be down to my last tenner again by the end of the month.

But still, you've got to try.

And desperate, hopeless optimist that I am, I keep trying.

Every now and then I get my very best business suit out of the depths of the ironing basket, pile on the slap, dust off my briefcase and go act like I'm a professional, cosmopolitan woman who is in control of her life, her career and her future.

The morning was planned like a military operation. Unfortunately, I forgot to let Corporal Callan (aged three) and Brigadier Brad (two) in on the strategy for the assault.

Husband was taking the kids out for the morning, so the plan was that he would drop me off for my meeting at nine o'clock and then collect me afterwards.

I set the alarm early to ensure I was up and organised before the boys. By seven o'clock I had blow-dried hair, a pressed suit and my agenda firmly focused in my mind.

Then it all went to pants. Literally.

Callan has been toilet-trained for months now, but he's not quite mastered the night-time toilet trips yet so he wears those much-advertised 'pull-up pants' at night. And, no, they don't make him want to do a conga with his pals, jump up and down with glee or dance around the room in just his knickers.

However, his life had been made complete the day before when we discovered the designer pull-up pant equivalent of Armani or Versace – pants with Buzz Lightyear on the front and back of them. He was beside himself with joy. Me, a little less so, because Cal's obsession with Buzz Lightyear has so far resulted in a compulsion to spontaneously jump from a great height shouting 'To infinity and beyond', two split lips, a dislocated elbow, suspected concussion and more bruising than Rocky at the end of ten rounds.

Anyway, he could barely sleep with excitement due to the new superhero addition to his night-time attire, and was still clutching the waistband when I went to wake him the next morning.

He immediately spotted that something was different. Jeans and stained T-shirt mum had been replaced by chic, suited, lipstick'd mum. Only one person could have accomplished this transformation. He gazed down at his pants in wonderment – it was amazing what Buzz Lightyear could do in just one shift.

I scooped both boys out of bed and deposited them at the breakfast table, holding them carefully in the under-arm position so that no snot or any other fluid could find its way from them to my smart togs.

With one eye on the clock, I airplane'd and choochoo'd their breakfast into them. So far so good. We were just about on schedule, with no surprises, minimal resistance (but Mum, I hate cornflakes, I want pizza for breakfast), and no casualties.

Then I was ambushed. By Buzz Lightyear.

I asked Callan to get undressed while I threw on Brad's clothes.

'Eh, nope.'

I paused, confused.

'What pet?'

'I'm not taking off my Buzz pants.'

'Come on honey, Mummy's in a big hurry today, you have to get ready to go.'

'Nope. Not taking off my Buzz pants.'

Hell. The enemy was engaged, and it was a five-inch-tall action figure with a space helmet and a jaw like David Coulthard.

It was an unanticipated hitch in the battle plan. I checked the clock. I had two choices: surrender, let him keep the pants on and make my meeting in the grown-up world on time, or face the challenge and risk being trounced.

I made a split-second decision, based on years of experience at the front line. As all parents know, once you get them out of nappies there's no going back. Weakness is fatal and likely to result in a return to lugging extra-large boxes of Pampers back from Asda and a twenty-pound-a-week dent in the shopping budget. I had to stick to my guns. Besides, he'd had the pants on all night and they were sagging down to his knees.

The way forward was clear: Buzz was coming off and nothing would deter me from my mission. Except, that is, a three-year-old boy who bolted to the bathroom like his Buzz-clad buttocks were on fire. And, of course, proceeded to lock the door.

We tried everything to get him out: bribery (new Scooby Doo video), blackmail (if you don't come out we're giving all your worldly goods to your wee brother) and coercion (come on, babe, show Buzz Lightyear how to open the door like a big boy). Twenty minutes, a husband who can burst a dodgy lock, and several tantrums (mostly mine) later, we finally broke through enemy lines. Buzz was cornered on two fronts, and eventually defeated, leaving only one furious wee boy who probably won't talk to his parents again until he hits puberty and needs pocket money. But, hey... for every pants debacle, there's a positive. Compared to the savage, danger-fraught minefield that is motherhood, breaking in to the movie industry should be a doddle. ◆

And the Number One Answer Is...

In a recent survey, 100 people were asked to list the things that irritate them most, and the winner was... stupid bloody surveys that ask people to list things.

Have scientists, the government and women's magazines got nothing better to do with their time than ask inane questions? Isn't there an ozone layer that needs patching up? Don't hospitals need some attention? Schools needing new books? Well, maybe, but first we'll just run off a potentially world-changing questionnaire asking 3,000 people what biscuit they like to dunk in their tea.

Now, usually I avoid surveys as I would, say, the bubonic plague or boob tubes, but this week there was one poll that genuinely intrigued and excited me. No, it wasn't the results of the survey that revealed that one in five blokes fake their orgasms (eh, I have questions) and that fifty-eight per cent of women do a Meg Ryan Special at the crucial moment.

And the Number One Answer Is...

Nor was I particularly interested in the result of another poll that concluded Britons spend an average of £169,000 during their lives on job costs like travel and lunches. Unless, of course, you're an MP, in which case you claim double that back.

I was even less impressed with the research done by a team at the University of St Andrews that revealed that women are just as grateful for cheap trinkets as they are for expensive diamonds, just as long as the gift is given with thought and love. Fab. Now as long as the love of your life dons a lopsided grin and recites a poem, he can palm you off with a genuine tin-plated, diamante love-heart ring from the Everything-For-A-Pound shop.

The study that did tweak my radar, however, was the survey of 25,000 seven- to eleven-year-olds that found more than half reckoned their mums could do anything. Yes, us marvellous matriarchs beat off stiff competition in the superhero stakes from icons like Superman, Spiderman and whoever invented Play-Doh.

In second place came fathers, their popularity increased no doubt by the young boys who took part in the survey and were impressed by dad's ability to multitask. My dearly beloved has an admirable ability to listen to me talking while simultaneously rolling his eyeballs to heaven.

And in third place came Harry Potter, that wee smug bloke who, unlike us mums, has to enlist the help of a wooden stick and a brainy (female) sidekick to conquer the impossible.

At two and three-quarters and four, my boys are below the age threshold for the survey, but I decided to boost my ever-flailing ego by checking that they concurred with the results.

'Boys, do you think Mummy can do anything in the whole wide world?' I asked with my sweetest, most grovelling grin. And, okay, I'll admit that the two packets of chocolate buttons I was dangling from each hand might have swayed them just slightly.

Still, they looked at each other hesitantly, in the manner of crime suspects who feared they were being lured into a trap by a master interrogator. After checking the escape routes and realising they were cornered, they nodded tentatively.

I should have stopped there, but come on... I'm a mother who doesn't get out much, I'm permanently knackered and dishevelled and I haven't had a cigarette now for nearly three weeks – I'm a real-life desperate housewife who'll clutch at any straw going for validation and appreciation.

'So what special things can I do then?' I cajoled, still piling on the saccharine with a fork-lift.

'Give magic kisses,' interjected Brad), referring to the cure for all ailments short of contagious diseases or anything relating to the bottom.

'That's right, sweetheart... and what else?'

'You can sing when you're upside down,' Cal exclaimed, his eyes never straying from the Buttons.

Yeah, Madonna eat your heart out. You might be bendy but I can belt out a catchy tune when I'm standing on my head. Although there is usually a bottle or two of full-strength Lambrusco involved in the preparation of that particular death-defying feat.

'And you can make the bell ring when dinner's ready.'

And that, I fear, is the reason us mums came out on top. Our tiny offspring still have the naïveté of youth and the unconditional love for their mothers that convinces them that the eardrum-shattering racket produced by the dangerous combination of a woman who can't cook, a tray of chicken dinosaurs, an oven and a smoke alarm is a little piece of magic. Harry Potter, eat your heart out. ◆

Father's Day

I always knew my family was unique. Last Sunday, we managed to disprove three commonly held theories: not all dads enjoy Father's Day, not all family days out are fun events, and not all mothers like shopping.

It started at the crack of dawn, when Callan jumped on husband's head brandishing a home-made card and asking if it was time for the cake yet. He hasn't quite mastered the differences between Father's Day, birthdays and Christmas. As far as he's concerned, if there are cards they come swiftly followed by an iced sponge in the shape of Santa or Bob the Builder.

As husband wiped the sleep from his eyes and waited expectantly for the usual parcel of socks and beer, I announced that this year his present was to be something much more special than a hastily wrapped token of our love and affection – we were going on a family day out to the shops where he could pick anything he wanted. As long as it cost less than twenty quid or could be purchased using the Argos vouchers I had left over from Christmas. A day out with the family? I think he'd have preferred a dozen Budweiser, but he put a brave face on it.

He didn't realise that I had an ulterior motive: I needed to indulge in a spot of panic-buying for myself. With two toddlers and a chronic lack of babysitters, my shopping sprees normally consist of me lying on the couch with a coffee, a Kit Kat and the Next Directory, but this was an emergency – I'd been invited to a posh lunch the next day and had just discovered that my 'smart functions' suit would no longer button up.

We trotted off to the nearest mall, where I diverted us into the first ladies' fashion shop we encountered. 'Just a quick look,' I promised, scanning the room for something that screamed 'suitable for posh lunch'. I spied a gorgeous suit and was flicking along the rail looking for my size (it's normally at the very back and labelled 'super-stretchy'), when I heard a strange clicking noise behind me. Husband had run off in one direction chasing Brad (two) and had momentarily taken his eye off Callan. Cal had seized the opportunity to ram his trainer-clad feet into a pair of kitten heels and was strutting supermodel-style across the shop, much to the horror of the assistants. I was mortified. I de-shoed him, bought the suit and vacated the premises before they made us pay for the footwear or called security.

I should have stopped there. But I'm a woman. I'm

programmed with a gene that compels me to check every other store within a mile radius to ensure there isn't something nicer than the thing I've just bought. And, besides, I needed a new bra to go under the suit. After two hours and a full-scale reconnaissance of every store in the centre, husband had the demeanour of a man on death row. Every time he suggested calling it a day I reminded him petulantly that we were only there in the first place to buy him a present. If I were in a Marvel comic, 'moan deflection' would be one of my superpowers.

On the way for a lunch stop, Callan spotted a golfing event that had been set up in the atrium, allowing kids to hit a few balls into a net. 'Can I have a shot, please?' he demanded. The 'please' did it. 'After lunch,' I promised. The minute the last morsel was cleared from our plates, he took off like a whippet. Naturally, I panicked and gave chase, hobbling along on blistered feet shouting, 'Stop that boy' to the bemused passers-by. By the time we caught up with him he was clutching a putter and teeing off. I was almost touched by the sweetness of it – until he realised that the putter looked quite like a Star Wars Lightsaber, adopted the posture of Luke Skywalker and thumped his wee brother.

'Look, forget my present, let's just go,' husband demanded over Brad's screams. 'Absolutely not,' I replied, steering him in the direction of those electrical shops that have lots of man-type gadgets. Fast forward two hours, husband still hadn't seen anything he wanted and I'd cunningly manoeuvred us into Markie's underwear department. It was chaos. None of the bras were in size order and the rails were so low that I had to squat as I rummaged for one that would fit. By this time, one of my sons whom I'll refrain from naming, was wearing a rosebud-pink bra on his head with the cups over his ears shouting, 'Look Mummy, I'm a Fimble.'

'There are a million bras here, how difficult can this be?' husband demanded in impatient tones.

I didn't have time to explain the complexities of gravity-defying underwear construction, because in a fit of boredom Brad suddenly launched himself at my squatting form, sending me sprawling across the floor. Another moment of dignity. Another swift exit.

I never did get my bra. Husband never did get his present. And I think the kids' faces are probably now on wanted posters in the shopping centre's security office.

'Do me a favour,' husband asked when we finally poured ourselves into the car. 'Next year, just buy me socks and beer.' ◆

Mind Your Manners

In the fourteenth century, an erudite gentleman by the name of William of Wykeham, coined the proverb 'Manners maketh man'. Impressed? I always knew that O Level history would come in handy.

Anyway, the truth of the saying does disturb me somewhat because, if manners are an intrinsic component of maturity, then I'm in danger of raising the Low equivalent of an episode of *Men Behaving Badly*.

When my boys grow up, I want them to be big, suave devils that could charm the pants off anyone. Not literally, of course. My precious angels won't be allowed to have sex until they're at least twenty-five, and only then with my express permission and after the potential suitor has been vetted by me for pure motivations and foolproof contraception.

Since the fundamental basis for charm and social skills is good manners, husband and I are already endeavouring to educate the boys in common courtesy. They're only two and four, so we're breaking them in gently and just going for the basics:

1. They have to say 'please' and 'thank you'.
2. No interrupting adults when adults are speaking.
3. No taking food or drinks without asking.
4. They must ask to be excused from the table after eating their dinner.

It's fair to say we're having a few teething problems, and not the kind that can be sorted by a quick dab of Bonjela and a dose of Calpol.

Callan is usually fairly consistent with his 'please' and 'thank you's. But lately, we've discovered that he carries the same rogue gene as his mother – the one that compels him to find his own bad, obtuse or inappropriate jokes absolutely hilarious.

Last week, we were in a pizza restaurant (the Low equivalent of nirvana) and a waitress was taking our order. 'I'd like fresh orange juice,' Callan announced.

My right eyebrow, the one that is responsible for maintaining order and discipline in our house, shot upwards at the speed of light. It's not an attractive look, but it usually gets the message across. 'What's the magic word?' I asked haughtily. Cal gave a sly glance at Brad. I recognised the signal – it's very subtle, but that quick look invariably accompanies them having a high-speed telepathic conversation to plan out a strategy for imminent mischief. The waitress was fidgeting so I knew I had to speed things up.

'What's the magic word?' I prompted again.

A cheeky smile, another impish peek at his brother, a deep breath, then in the loudest voice his wee lungs could support, he announced 'PUMP!'

At which point, Callan, Brad and everyone at the eight tables within earshot collapsed into fits of giggles.

Just my luck to have spawned a comedian.

Still, at least it's better than Brad's efforts. Brad, aka Wee Chunky, isn't the most eloquent of toddlers and has developed a particular fondness for the word 'okay'. Thus, reminders about manners tend to go along the lines of:

'Say "please", Brad.'

Brad: 'Okay.'

'No, not "okay", "please". You have to say "please" if you want something.'

Brad: 'Okay.'

'No, "please". Not "okay". Say "please".'

Brad: 'Okay.'

It can go on for hours. It could be worse. His one-favourite-word vocabulary could consist only of a loud, proud 'pump'.

We're not having much more success with the concept of waiting in turn to speak. Both boys were like those really annoying ascending ringtones that you get on mobile phones. If husband and I were talking, they'd interject with a fairly calm, 'Mummy, I want a biscuit/juice/toy/video/push on the swing/all-inclusive week in the most expensive suite in the Disneyland Hotel.' (Delete as applicable.)

If we had the temerity to ignore them and continue our conversation (which of course was usually about global warming, international economic strategies or the plight of the Amazonian rainforest and never, ever a trivial verbal joust about such mundane things as whose turn it was to put out the wheelie bin) then the boys would just repeat the same sentence over and over again, getting louder with ever utterance. We'd be forced to give in when the decibel level threatened to shatter the windows.

So, as soon as we thought they could comprehend it, we introduced the concept of saying 'excuse me' then waiting until they were asked to continue. They haven't quite mastered it yet. Instead, they now just shout 'excuse me' in gradually increasing volume until they reach the noise level of an outdoor rock concert.

Rule number three? Yesterday, I twice walked into the kitchen to see baseball boots attached to toddler-sized legs dangling out of the biscuit cupboard – a definite health hazard as the biscuit cupboard is an upper-wall unit. The only way for a four-year-old to scale that height is to climb up onto a bar stool then jump onto the kitchen worktop and balance there precariously while trying to manoeuvre the cupboard door open and locate Jaffa Cakes. I can feel another trip to accident and emergency looming.

And as for asking to be excused from the table, if we could

get them to sit there long enough without having an urgent compulsion to lie on the floor, dance like Michael Flatley, or wander off to the toilet at five-minute intervals, then perhaps we'd get the chance to try that one out.

Oh, the sheer weariness of it all. Manners may maketh man, but for mum? Permission to leave the table, please. ◆

Terror Tots

I pride myself on being a fairly fearless member of the female species. I'm the woman who spent several years standing at the doors of Glasgow nightclubs, knocking back anyone who had drooled on their outerwear or had the temerity to wear white socks with black shoes. I've flown EasyJet and survived the scrum of death between the boarding gate and the aeroplane. I've even had a Brazilian wax. Once.

But I'm about to be subjected to the one event that terrifies me to the extent that my hands start to vibrate like an Ann Summers' party bag at the very thought of it: playgroup duty.

Two-year-old Brad is about to join the same playgroup that his older brother once terrorised. It's a wonderful environment where they focus on the positive interaction between the children and on developing their creative skills. The session is managed by two lovely and ever-patient playgroup teachers, supplemented every week by at least three mothers.

And woe, oh woe, it'll be another exercise in proof that

when God gave out 'coping with kiddie' genes, I was down the pub with the over-eighteens clutching a Bacardi Breezer and a ciggie.

The irony is that it's one of my girlfriends who does the duty rota. You'd think that she would cut me a bit of slack. I've offered her everything from my left kidney to the entire contents of my bank account (enough to buy her, oh, at least a curry and a DVD for a wild, wanton Saturday night), and still she won't let me off the hook. She says she's doing it for my own good. I reckon it's for the entertainment value of seeing me fraught, harassed and begging for mercy, surrounded by people who come up to my knees. If this were Roman times, they'd sack the gladiators, free the lions and just put me in an arena with a bunch of three-year-olds instead.

Apparently, most of the other mothers view their monthly shift as an absolute joy, a treat that allows them to share in the playgroup experience with their offspring.

So why do I feel more out of my depth than a Premier League footballer at a monogamy convention?

I think what causes the overwhelming anxiety is the sheer responsibility of it; the intense pressure to be on my very best behaviour for a whole three hours, in the presence of the most hypercritical, brutally honest and super-observant members of our race. Give me a room full of souped-up ravers or a boardroom of city-slicker executives any day of the week. At least they don't burst into tears when I dole out plain digestives instead of Jammy Dodgers.

It's just a whole different stratosphere from handling your own children. When my two have an altercation rivalling the last Tyson/Lennox bout, it's easy to prise them apart, put them in separate corners and warn them not to come out until they can shake hands without it turning into a sumo bout.

The joy of parenting is that I am at all times free to resort to threats, bribery or negotiation in the name of discipline. It's amazing what a warning of withholding Jaffa Cakes can achieve.

But when it's someone else's children, they have to be treated with a sunny disposition and kid gloves at all times.

I have a recurring nightmare that one of the little darlings goes home after I've been looking after him and informs his mother that, 'Brad's mummy taught me a new word today: arse!'

So, tomorrow I'll spend three hours smiling (if a little dementedly), acting like the epitome of serenity and doing my damndest to be pure of mouth. I'll join in the singing, even though I don't know the words to 'Miss Molly Had a Dolly' (most of our songs are ones we made up ourselves, consisting almost entirely of inappropriate references to bodily functions, which my two Neanderthals find hilarious).

I'll referee when Child A coshes Child B with Bob the Builder's hammer. I'll clean up the mess when a receptacle of milk is hurled at speed because the cup is 'the wrong colour'. I'll valiantly manage to conceal the fact that I'm counting the minutes until I can return to adult civilisation. And I'll try my bloody best not to swear once. Not even under my breath.

It'll be my biggest achievement since childbirth.

And a month later I'll get to do it all over again. Although, I think I might be busy that morning. Flying EasyJet to Brazil for a spot of waxing. ◆

It's Criminal...

Picture the scene: twenty years from now, I'm sitting on my sofa, sipping a port and lemon while I watch television. I'm wearing the latest fashion – a pink Teflon housecoat and a furry big slipper that covers both feet. I've had so many facelifts that my hips are sitting somewhere above my inflatable neck cushion, but you can't see that I'm upset about it because I've overdone the Botox again. I turn to my husband (I'd love to think it'll be the same one I've got now, but guaranteed he'll have left me by then for a woman who doesn't think all food comes frozen) and ask him to turn the channel over.

'No way,' he moans, '*Match of the Day* is on and they're giving Gary Lineker his bus pass.'

'Aw, go on,' I plead. 'I want to see if our Callan is on the other side.'

Reluctantly, he turns it over, just as the show I want to see is about to start. Yes, I'm sure my oldest son Callan is going to be in the starring role.

So what programme has got me on the edge of my big slipper?

Is Callan the sexiest Scottish Bond since Sir Sean? Is he addressing the nation in his role as Prime Minister?

The opening credits fade and suddenly the face of a geriatric Nick Ross fills the screen.

'Welcome to *Crimewatch.*'

Yes, I'm getting seriously worried about my firstborn son. A few months ago, I read a report claiming that criminal tendencies could be spotted as far back as early childhood – apparently it's all to do with brain function and social habits. To be honest, I filed it in my great big box marked 'complete tosh' – along with the recent revelations that eating loads of chocolate makes you want to have more sex (armed with three selection boxes and a family-sized Dairy Milk, I've extensively researched this subject and it's definitely not true).

However, I'm beginning to wonder if there's an element of truth in the claims and, if there is, then I fear that *Crimewatch* beckons. You see, my gorgeous firstborn, aged four and two weeks, wants to be a 'baddie'. Gone are the days when he was Buzz Lightyear, saving the universe and making three trips a week to casualty because he'd flown off the top step again. Now, he's Doctor Octopus, nemesis of Spiderman and the biggest threat to our planet since the eradication of the ozone layer.

I first noticed the change in his objects of hero-worship

a few months ago. We had a few of his friends over for tea, and the superheroes were busily banishing the world of all evil from their nerve centre in my hall cupboard. Batman was there, complete with one of my best black towels serving as a cape. Spiderman was wearing my favourite red leggings circa 1985. And Superman had somehow managed to wangle on his Postman Pat pants over his jeans.

'And who are you?' I asked Callan, slightly disconcerted that he had my mop bucket over his head.

'Darth Vader.'

Oh. It was his first outing to the dark side. But I don't think he's left it since. Some weeks later we were cuddled up on the couch watching *Scooby Doo*. Batman, Robin and their usual entourage of villains must have been hard up for cash because they were making a special guest appearance with those pesky kids.

'I want to be like him!' Callan yelled halfway through. Ah, my boy was back on the right side of the law, I thought with relief. 'Which one, Batman or Robin?'

'No, Mummy,' he replied with utter disdain. 'I want to be the Joker.'

Nope, I wasn't laughing. Nor was I amused when he demanded a few days later that his name be changed. In this household, we now have Mr and Mrs Low, and their children, Brad and Doctor Doom.

And if Brad (aka 'Me Too', because he copies everything his brother does) follows suit, then I'll have to face up to the fact that my hall cupboard is now the breeding ground for the next generation of dastardly criminals.

Crimewatch, if my pink Teflon housecoat and a furry big slipper go missing, I'll be in touch. ◆

Porcelain Thrones and Megaphones ››››

Ready, Aim, Fire...

If reincarnation does in fact exist, can I please make a special request to come back as Julia Roberts? The lovely Julia was pictured last week leaving a Pilates class with her six-week-old twins. It was a sweet, precious and intimate snapshot of domestication: just Julia, her husband, her babies, and an army of helpers so large it could have invaded a small country.

Ladies, how many things are wrong with that scenario? Well, for a start, when my babies were six weeks old I couldn't find my way out of my dressing gown, never mind into a wee Juicy Couture tracky for a jaunt up the leisure centre.

Secondly, the gilded A-lister was partaking in the practice of evil: an exercise class. Doesn't she know that there's an unwritten rule among the sisterhood (or should that be motherhood)? For at least two months – or in my case, years – after childbirth we're supposed to milk the memory of the physical trauma we've inflicted on our bodies by endeavouring at all times to have our feet in an elevated position and our mouths in close proximity to a chocolate snack. It's the law.

And thirdly – and this is the real killer – Team Julia were carrying everything for her. She didn't have a bulk-size box of Huggies strapped to her back. There were no bottles of milk dribbling up the arm of her jumper as she attempted to juggle baby, bag and feeding equipment. And she wasn't within projectile-vomit range of either of her newborns.

That's not motherhood, it's a holiday.

While Miss Roberts gets the five-star, deluxe version of motherhood, this week I've been subjected to the self-catering, dodgy plumbing and offensive odours version. In the latest episode of my oh-so-glamorous life, I decided it was time for almost-three-year-old Brad to lose the nappies.

For those of you who are just tucking into a wee cup of tea and a bacon roll, I'll spare you the details. But let's just say that disinfectant spray became my very best friend. On the first day of Brad's nappy liberation, I spent the whole time on my hands and knees contemplating puddles. Who knew children that small could store that much water? My second-born son is the toddler equivalent of a Saharan camel.

By lunchtime, I was soaked, exhausted and could feel the thud of my will to live tunnelling to freedom.

Worse, Brad was getting thoroughly sceptical about my promise that 'Big Boys Pants' would give him supernatural powers. Hopefully, one of which would be the ability to control his bladder.

Never has my familiar prima-donna war cry, 'I bet Jackie Collins doesn't have to put up with this pish!' had a more literal meaning.

At four o'clock, wet, smelling of Eau de Sewer and covered in stains that I didn't even want to think about, I speed-dialled the husband for moral support. It didn't go well.

'Hi, honey, having a good day?' he had the absolute temerity to ask.

A GOOD DAY? Aaargh!

Yes, I know the poor man was only being polite but in my pee-soaked brain that somehow became a patronising comment from a smug bloke sitting in a comfy chair, in a civilised office, having conversations with other adults that consisted of words of more than one syllable, all the while partaking of hot and cold running bloody cappuccinos.

How dare he!

I slammed the phone down in disgust. I didn't say I was rational. I'm a mother of two toddlers – that's not in the job description.

Next day, over breakfast I was mulling over my dilemmas for the day: whether donning waterproof clothing was an overreaction, whether Dettox was available in gallon-size tubs and how to convince my husband that we didn't, in fact, require a marriage guidance counsellor. So absorbed was I in my woes that I didn't notice that Brad had left the table for a far comfier seat – one atop the porcelain throne. Yes, my wee angel had finally mastered the concept of waste management.

Because I Said So

Overjoyed, I had an irresistible compulsion to call the *One O'Clock* News team to announce the thrilling news: Brad was toilet-trained. There's only one downside – his aim isn't brilliant. But then, I've never met a grown man who doesn't share that problem, so I'm guessing it's a gender thing.

There's obviously a limit to the supernatural powers of Big Boy Pants. ◆

Jamie's Bitchin

My boys are threatening mutiny. They can't decide whether to call Childline or the NSPCA. Apparently, I'm up there with Cruella de Vil and whoever invented face-washing, since I took the monumental decision to banish their favourite pet forever. Yes, the chicken dinosaur is no longer a cherished member of the Low family. Thank you, Saint Jamie of the Immaculate School Dinners.

I am so glad that television series is finished. Don't get me wrong, it was an admirable crusade on the part of Mr bleep bleep Oliver to highlight the scandalous 37p that's allocated for our children's school lunches. Disgraceful. In my day (when a balanced diet was equal amounts of salt and vinegar), that would only have bought two packets of Worcester sauce crisps and a donut from the baker's across the road.

He has also done a splendid job in raising awareness of the rubbish that's in processed food. It seems that we can now call a pile of stodge a chicken nugget as long as it drove past KFC on the way to the supermarket frozen-food aisle.

However, if I'm completely honest, my enthusiasm for Mr Oliver's revelations is tempered somewhat with a good old helping of guilt. Oh, groan. As if, according to whatever survey is in the headlines this week, I shouldn't have enough of that to go around already. If I'm not damaging my kids by sending them to childcare while I'm working, then the fact that I'm letting them live near mobile phone masts, in a polluted environment, with American fast-food joints and the Cartoon Network, is probably scarring them for life.

In our house, as always, we have a conflict of opinions at mealtimes. In the red corner (it's actually bland beige, but artificial colourings E45, E89, E101 have been added to make it more aesthetically appealing) is four-year-old Callan. This boy wants jelly for breakfast, sweets for lunch, and Ben & Jerry's chocolate chip ice cream for dinner. If we left him alone in a sweet shop, within three minutes it would look like it had been raided by crack-addled youths. It's taken years of bribery and negotiation (loosely translated as blatant threats – eat up your cucumber or Bob the Builder is taking early retirement) to gently persuade him to eat a balanced diet. And now he does. Almost. Wholemeal toast, yoghurt and fruit in the morning, healthy sandwich and more fruit for lunch and, well, then it all goes a bit Turkey Twizzler. His dinner plate always has two vegetables on it but they're usually perched next to a medley of summer Smiley Faces and a freshly roasted, hand-reared, mignon of chicken dinosaur. Or pizza. Or finger of fish.

In the greens corner, however, my almost-three-year-old, Brad, is another kettle of organic cod. He refuses to eat sweets, chocolate, ice cream, cake... anything, in fact that's not a fruit, vegetable, or bread. Sounds great in theory, but it is a worry that he would sooner pull his toenails out with Bob the Builder's magic pliers than eat any form of protein. Except, of course, the much-revered chicken dinosaur.

Now, like many likeminded parents, I was happy to acquiesce to their foibles, mainly because, after a hard day's graft, I strangely never had a notion to cook organic tofu with flambéed broccoli from scratch.

But that's been changed by equal measures of enlightenment and guilt. And a sneaky premonition of *School Dinners*, series seven – the one where Jamie comes to a primary school in Glasgow in 2008, holds up a leek in front of a class of kids and asks them what it is.

A wee blonde called Callan, no doubt sitting in the front row so that the teacher can keep an eye on him, shoots his hand into the air, yelling, 'I know, I know.'

'Go on then, pukka, pukka, bleep, bleep geezer, tell us what it is.'

'A Lightsaber!'

The very thought has inspired (spelt S-H-A-M-E-D) me into conjuring up fresh meals from now on. Last night, out came Annabel Karmel's book of kids' recipes, and I rustled up a plate of cannelloni that was designed to look like four human shapes lying in a bed. I'm sure that's illegal in some countries.

It took an hour and a half to cook, but it looked great, it smelled great and it tasted great. Except to two wee boys who were still in mourning for their dinosaurs and refused to touch it. But I'm not giving up. Oh no, it's paella tonight and they'd better eat it or bye bye Bob.

Jamie, you should be proud. And if you get a call from Childline, don't worry about it… it was caused by two mighty miffed wee boys who've just discovered that chicken dinosaurs are extinct. ◈

The Mother of
All Jobs

Could you imagine the situations vacant ad for motherhood?

Wanted: Female to work from home. Must be able to cook to GCSE level (Great Chips, Sausages and Eggs) and be qualified above HNC (House Needs Cleaning) in Environmental Services. Vivid imagination and the capacity to turn cardboard into countless hours of amusement is essential. Should be prepared to work eighteen-hour days (overtime unpaid), often in hazardous conditions involving noxious fumes and unsanitary fluids. Will be responsible for budgetary control, travel arrangements, entertainment co-ordination, health plans and behaviour management. The ability to work under pressure is mandatory, as is a talent for diffusing stressful situations without the use of audible profanity. Must be a skilled educator with the patience of a religious icon and have the capacity to remain cheerful despite urban warfare, rejection and PMS. Sense of humour required, as is a talent for endless repetition of commands and activities. Basic nursing skills, experience of high-level negotiations, and a demonstrable track record of peacekeeping in volatile situations would be an advantage.

Please note that this is a voluntary position, but lodgings and uniform of stain-resistant fabrics and shapeless fleece jumper is provided.

Somehow, I don't think they'd need to call in crowd-control officers down at the job centre.

Of course, it's all worth it for our darling delinquents (or is that just mine?), and none of us would change a single moment of our child-rearing days. Actually, that's not true – I'd happily skip the whole 'potty' period and move straight on to unreasonable tantrums and demands.

One of the biggest perks of the job, though, is Mother's Day. This Sunday we'll have a whole twenty-four hours dedicated to showing us how indispensable we are and rewarding us for 364 days of unpaid labour. Commercial nonsense? Most definitely. But it's in the motherhood code of behaviour that we must milk to the death any amount of sentimental adulation and fawning praise that's going because we know it doesn't happen very often. And, besides, you can't beat soggy

Cornflakes in bed and a card made out of old newspaper and string.

I do, however, have one complaint – the prezzies are about as useful as Jimmy Choos in a swamp.

I could quite happily live without another bunch of Esso's finest blooms. My hips could survive without another box of Quality Street. I want practical presents (however, dear husband, if you confuse this last statement with a plea for any form of kitchen utensil you may lose your life on Sunday).

I want things that make my daily life easier. So I'm putting together a list of invaluable tools and inventions that every mother should have. Manufacturers, shop bosses and marketing bods, please take note.

Top of the list is a megaphone. This is inspired by the fact that my boys, aged four and almost three, have already acquired that man-skill that allows them to tune out all verbal communication that doesn't involve the subjects of play, sport, food, television or treats.

'Boys, can you put your clothes in the washing basket please?'
Ignored.
'Right, guys, it's bath time.'
Glazed over, non-responsive.
'Who'd like ice cream?'
Two scud missiles shoot to the freezer. My youngest doesn't even like ice cream, but he's still in the 'copying everything his brother does' phase.

This extraordinary talent has resulted in recurring throat

problems for me as I inevitably end up repeating my request until I'm shrilling like a fishwife in a voice so high-pitched that only the neighbourhood dogs can hear me.

Next on the list of motherhood must-haves is a satellite navigation system for shoes, gloves and hats. If we could pinpoint those items at a moment's notice, just think how much extra time we'd have in the day – almost enough to replace the toilet seat to a 'down' position every time it's been left up.

And how about a car-wash-type contraption for children? Just stand them on a conveyor belt and two minutes later they come out of the other side, washed, dried and dressed in pristine pyjamas.

Personally, I'd also appreciate a course in acrobatics and contortion that will give me the ability to get a restful night's sleep on the six inches of mattress that are left after the entire population of the household have climbed into my bed.

And, finally, I want a secret override device for the television remote control.

This has no practical application to my motherhood duties, but it would give me hours of fun watching husband's puzzled and horrified face when Sky Sports repeatedly flicks over to reruns of *Cagney and Lacey*.

Oops, forgot to put that in the ad – the undoubted bonus of being able to indulge in childish, nonsensical behaviour whenever it takes your fancy.

Just another little perk to go alongside the soggy Cornflakes in bed and the card made of string. ◆

Excess Baggage

Suntan lotion? Check. Lilos? Check. First aid kit? Check. Waterwings tested for punctures? Check. Emergency numbers on speed-dial? Check.

Those wickedly indulgent four little summer S-words were almost within my grasp – Sun, Sea, Sand and S… Okay, I admit it. Much as I want to appear like a wild rock and roll chick who can still get raunchy with the best of them, all I could think about was the giddy joy that I wouldn't be burning the midnight oil over my laptop for a fortnight, so I was sure to catch up on some SLEEP.

However, at 1.30 on the morning of the day we were due to set off on our last-minute break to Cyprus, I was drowning in the middle of a sea of rubber inflatables (of the non-pornographic variety, Gran), with the fraught demeanour of a mother who has less than twenty-four hours to get everything organised for two weeks away with two under-fives.

Because I Said So

Other families seem to sail through it – all rosy cheeks, kiss-me-quick hats and jolly renditions of 'We're All Going on a Summer Holiday' as they bound up the aeroplane steps. We, on the other hand, were working up to our holiday with all the serenity and tranquillity of the Tweenies on crack.

Although, while that didn't diminish the fact that I was rapt with excitement about our first fortnight in the sun since 1999BC (before children), it did reinforce the sad reality that I was clearly out of practise. I used to be able to throw a few things in a suitcase and take off for a spontaneous break with ten minutes' notice. Now I was pretty close to demanding a government consultation and strategy team to work out if fifteen cans of insect repellent was a tad excessive, if suntan cream for kids came in factor 650 and whether or not Glasgow Airport had Lambrusco in the Duty Free.

I was also discovering that travelling en masse requires the logistical planning of a moon landing. I'd spent weeks (okay, a couple of hours on the Internet but I'm going for maximum exaggeration/sympathy points here) researching and planning the trip, all the kids' new togs were piled up beside me and the Ambre Solaire was already leaking onto my beach towels.

The brown hyperventilation bag was on standby as I mentally ran through my to-do list. I still had to pack two cases (the summer equivalent of fitting nine elephants in a mini), do a few hours' work, strip three beds, clean the house, find a bikini that fitted, and lose three stone. A doddle.

Still, at least my boys were fast asleep and would be well rested for their big day. All three of them. Yes, husband was having a wee early night while I aged ten years with the stress of organising two weeks' supplies for a family of four. Bless him. I paused as I packed the Ladyshave. He'll never know how close he came to spending two weeks on a Cyprus beach with a five o'clock shadow. On his legs.

A few hours later, after grabbing a brief forty winks, I packed the kids off to nursery and maniacally worked my way through the rest of my to-do list.

By mid-afternoon I was just about organised and all set for the final stage of Operation Beach Bum. It seemed like a foolproof plan. Pick up the kids from nursery and check in for our flight four hours early. Since we only live twenty minutes away from the airport, this would give us time to drive home, have a leisurely tea and shower, allow the boys to have a wee nap and we'd all arrive back at the airport fed, watered, refreshed and ready to belt out Cliff Richard's greatest hits at the departure gate.

Ah, it sounded like a great plan. Unfortunately, it didn't take into account a two-hour hold-up at the check-in desk. The result was a mad dash home to grab the carry-on luggage, with no time to eat, change or nap, and in the midst of it all I lost my make-up bag, hairbrush, composure and the factor 650.

So, if you were one of the unfortunate souls who was stuck next to an un-showered mother, a huffy husband and two hungry, hyperactive kids all the way to Paphos last week, I'd like to extend my sincere apologies for introducing you to the other four little summer S-words: Stress, Smells, Sulks and Strops. ◆

The Sun is Out...

The sun is out, the sky is blue, and the only cloud spoiling the view is the one puffing skywards from the bloke on the next sun lounger's cigarette. No, I haven't become a neo-nicotine fascist – just because I've been a smoke-free zone since New Year doesn't mean I'm going all evangelical about the scourge of ciggies. In fact, it's the opposite. My subconscious has obviously realised that this is my first ever non-smoking holiday and, from the moment we landed at Paphos airport, I've had a compelling urge to mug anyone sporting a packet of Silk Cut. Since the inside of a Cypriot clink doesn't hold much appeal, I've been mentally counting up the contents of my beach bag and I'm trying to summon up the courage to ask Smoky Joe to swap me a ciggy for two bottles of suntan lotion, a broken camera, half a watermelon and a lilo.

Still, at least my new daily activities of football, volleyball, water polo and trying to remain at least fifty yards away from perfectly toned model-types in bikinis at all times is a bit of a distraction from the cravings. Although I could do without my sons' aversion to suntan lotion that has me doing a Sally Gunnell around the pool five times a day, clutching a bottle of Ambre Solaire and shouting, 'Stop right there or you're grounded for ever!'

Waltons. Us. Hard to tell the difference.

I've learned so many other new things about my wee darlings since we got here. For example, let's talk pants.

In mothering school they do not warn you that small boys will fight to the death over a pair of pants. When buying the holiday undies, I made the fatal mistake of splashing out on multipacks with five pairs each of the following knick-knacks: Power Rangers, Spiderman, Batman and Star Wars. What I didn't realise is that there's a secret action figure hierarchy, and that Spiderman, Batman and the Power Rangers have been relegated to the superhero subs bench. Apparently, no fashion-conscious toddler will venture to the kiddie disco in anything other than briefs from the Dark Side. Every night, our apartment has resounded with the thuds of wrestling, interjected by wails of 'I want the Storm Troopers and I want them now!'

Neither did I realise that my youngest son, three-year-old Brad (now known as Pledge, for reasons that will become clear), had inherited his father's obsession with neatness and order to such an extreme degree. He's always been a tidy wee soul – the only three-year-old I know who makes his bed, puts his clothes in the washing and does the dishes after every meal. If you're the mother of a little girl between two and five – especially if she's gorgeous and has a bulging piggy bank – then feel free to send a photo and details of your child. I'm open to an arranged marriage and, trust me, he's such a catch that your girl will thank you in twenty years' time when she's sitting with her feet up doing her nails and he's hoovering around her.

However, he's starting to worry me. Yesterday, I took him and his brother to one of those little tourist supermarkets that sells everything from fruit juice to flippers and, in a moment of sunstroke-induced weakness, let them loose with the promise that they could have 'one little toy'. Cal came back with a snorkel, two tennis bats and a dinghy, while Brad returned sporting a big grin, a box of Daz and a packet of black bin bags. I think he's been secretly brainwashed by Kim and Aggie.

The scariest holiday revelation, though, may scar me for life. I've discovered that my boys can pick up any song in five minutes and repeat it throughout every waking moment for days on end. It started when we were roused from our slumbers on day two by the joyous strains of a particularly irritating anthem that they learned from those twisted kids' entertainers.

Dear Lord, make it stop.

Nicotine may be dangerous, Storm Troopers may be a tad sinister. Kim and Aggie's secret lovechild may be downright terrifying. But the true root of all evil? The sick git who wrote 'Aaaaagaaaa Do Do Do'.

Next year, I might just go for that week in the clink with a packet of Silk Cut. ◆

Stick 'Em Up...

I've learned some valuable lessons about family life in the last couple of weeks. The whole 'Jude Law – affair with the nanny' debacle has taught me that, if I'm ever rich enough to employ a resident childcare expert (oh, I can dream), I should make sure that she looks like Mrs Doubtfire.

I've learned that Supernanny's naughty corner technique is useless in open spaces.

And those photos of forty-one-year-old mother of two Elle McPherson, looking like a goddess in nothing but a cowboy hat and a bikini have reinforced my belief that Yummy Mummies should be outlawed.

Okay, so I'm bitter and twisted, but only because my one attempt at cowboy chic went downhill faster than Lance Armstrong on a Chopper. On holiday last month, I tried out a natty wee Texan number.

'What do you think?' I asked husband, as I twirled in a Stetson. 'Trendy, sexy and alluring?'

'Hoss from *Bonanza*,' was the reply.

Dejected, I decided just to buy them for the kids and kill two birds with one stone: prevent any risk of sunburn while allowing them to impersonate a fine, upstanding, positive role model – Woody, the good-guy cowboy sheriff from *Toy Story*.

It was all going so well until my youngest decided to plump for a life of intergalactic crime.

I took Callan, four, and Brad, three to the cinema. I walked in with two wee cowboys, strutting their stuff like they were en route to the Alamo. Aw, they were gorgeous. But at some point during the movie Brad had a juice, a banana and a personality transplant. As we were leaving, I handed over his headgear.

'Here you go honey, put your hat on.'

'No. I don't want to be Woody. I'm the Evil Emperor Zurg.'

I was stunned – this is the child who is normally the poster boy for reasonable behaviour.

'But, but, but … Come on hon, put your hat on.'

I plonked his hat on his napper, as I took his hand to cross the car park. I was so busy checking left and right that it wasn't until I got to the car that I realised that the hat had been abandoned halfway across.

I immediately adopted phase one of my tried and tested disciplining technique – possible only because I've been too skint to get the Botox done this summer: the raised eyebrow of warning. I was rewarded with crossed arms, a defiant stare and a petted lip that reached his cowboy boots.

Panic set in. Exposed area, not a naughty corner in sight and at least twenty people watching what was fast turning into the biggest stand-off outside of a cowboy flick.

I crouched down to his eye level, and in my very best serious mummy voice said, 'Come on, we're going back over there and we're going to pick up that hat.'

'No.'

'Yes we are, Brad. Right now.'

'No.'

'We're going to go back over there and you're going to pick up that hat.'

'N…' You get the picture.

Patience may be a virtue and good things may come to those who wait, but ten minutes and about three hundred point blank refusals later, the Evil Emperor Zurg was still more stubborn than cellulite. But surrender wasn't an option. I took a deep breath and reminded myself that I'm a mature, intelligent adult who is more than capable of coming up with a mature, intelligent way to deal with a three-foot sheriff with an identity crisis.

'We're going to pick up that hat right now or your *Toy Story* DVD is going in the bin.'

For the first time, I registered hesitation. The lip started to tremble. The feet started to tap. A wee hand closed a little tighter around mine and there were the very beginnings of a nod.

Victory! I straightened up, not an easy task when you've

lost all feeling in your legs, looked left, looked right and…
just as we were about to take that first triumphant step, a
big white van came into the car park and rolled right over
the hat.

Cue floods of tears, uncontrollable sobs, and a wail so
piercing that three people rushed out to switch off their car
alarms.

Still, on the bright side, I may have a three-year-old with
no hat, but we'll never be short of a frisbee.

More lessons in life: patience is not a virtue, good things
don't come to those who wait, and wherever I lay my hat?
That's where some bloody big transit van will run over it. ◆

Big Mother is Watching

It was another moment of dignity. The atmosphere had been light but reserved as the crowd moved reverentially along, adults and children alike locked in gentle chatter fuelled by mutual curiosity and, in some instances, mild apprehension.

Suddenly it was all too much.

As we turned a corner, a bubble of excitement worked its way from my stomach to my mouth and, without warning, inhibitions or respect for the eardrums of others, a cosmic intervention gave me the vocal chords of Joe Pasquale with a helium habit.

'Look, look!' I screeched to my four-year-old son. 'Callan, it's… your COAT PEG!!!'

The startled crowd in the hallway suddenly hushed as many eyes swivelled in our direction. At which point my super-cool wee boy got a raging beamer, slapped a hand to his forehead and learned a valuable fact of life. That his mother had been put on earth to mortify him at every possible opportunity.

This was the worst one yet. Worse than the time I insisted on cleaning him up with a baby wipe after a big boy tackled him on the rugby park. Worse than the time he was playing in goals on a rainy afternoon and I stood over him with an umbrella. It even overshadowed the misguided attempt to cut his hair while he was asleep that resulted in him spending a fortnight looking like he was related to a native tribe of North America commonly known as Mohicans.

In my defence, my irrational state of overexcitement had been caused by the momentousness of the occasion – my firstborn's tour of the primary school that he'll start going to in August.

School!

Where have the years gone? It seems like no time at all since I watched that blue line appear on the stick. Or should I say, sticks. After six years of fertility treatment it took fourteen tests, an ultrasound and a sworn affidavit from a gynaecologist for me to even begin to contemplate that I was finally up the duff. And it wasn't until I'd experienced the dual indignities of piles and trying to manoeuvre a body the size of a garden shed up the baby aisle in Marks & Spencer that I fully believed it was true.

And now, a five-minute blur of toddlerdom later, I'm measuring my firstborn up for school shoes and trying to ensure his behaviour is on the non-karate side of Power

Ranger by convincing him that the lampposts and fence around the school contain invisible cameras that'll allow me to watch him at all times.

He'll be easy to spot in the playground – he'll be the one that's shouting, 'I didn't mean it, Mum, honest!' to a six-foot wall of chain link.

I know some mothers are filled with trepidation at the thought of their offspring taking their first steps to education, independence and detention, but I can honestly say that with Cal I'm all out of frantic worry and hand-wringing. It'll be a different story in two years' time when Brad, his shy, timid, wary little brother, makes the same journey. When that happens, I will undoubtedly have been involved in a freak chemical accident that results in Brad and I being bonded at the ankle until at least the October break.

Cal, however, is an extroverted, sociable wee soul who loves to entertain. Give him an audience and he'll be on a table belting out the theme tune from *Spiderman*, while tap dancing in my only pair of decent high heels – the ones normally kept for special occasions and cheering me up when I've got PMT.

So, instead of locking himself away with the Yellow Pages and frantically ringing round therapists who specialise in separation anxiety, he's revelling in the prospect of being with his pals all day, getting decent grub at lunchtime, followed by a game of footie and a sing-song in the afternoon.

Still, I've no doubt that there will be tears, tantrums and a sleepless night before he dons that uniform for the first time. But enough about how I'll feel.

Cal will be absolutely fine. And if he does suffer from any pangs of loneliness, he can always go have a wee chat to a lamppost.

Somehow, though, I think he'll be too busy with the fundamentals of his education: reading his books, spelling his words and counting his blessings that he's got eight hours every day when his mother can't give him a beamer. ◆

On Yer Bike

There are loads of occupations that have their busiest times in the summer. Deckchair salesmen. Lifeguards. And north of Hadrian's Wall it's a great time for umbrella manufacturers.

But this weekend I realised that there's another, less obvious, field that must see a sharp upturn in business: the osteopath. Just go down to any local park and you'll see dozens of parents hobbling around clutching their backs and wincing. They're all suffering from an excruciating medical complaint brought on by indulgence in an extreme sport: bike training. As soon as summer comes, the stabilisers are off. The result is a posse of preschoolies wobbling up the pavements on their Barbie bikes, swiftly followed by whatever parent lost the toss of the coin, bent double, clutching Evel Knievel's bike seat and running as fast as their flip-flops will take them.

Husband and I have been dreading the two-wheel challenge for months. Cal, may only be four, but he has the adventure cravings of Buzz Lightyear on Buckfast. He announced last week that he wants to go mountain climbing. Where did we get him from? It's not as if the rest of the family are hyped-up adrenalin junkies – my idea of a death-defying stunt is waxing my legs without a general anaesthetic.

I know we should be thrilled that we've given birth to a child so fearless, but somehow it doesn't seem like such a good quality when he's doing triple-back somersaults off the roof of the garage.

Last weekend, though, we realised that if we didn't take the stabilisers off then Cal would do it himself. And last time he managed to get hold of the toolbox he dismantled the bathroom sink. So, with much plucking up of courage and a rising feeling of impending doom, the stabilisers were abandoned. Fear in our hearts, we trundled down to our local school playground, having already taken every emergency precaution: the Southern General had been alerted to have the casualty team on standby, the first aid kit was within arm's reach, and Cal was decked out in elbow pads, kneepads, a padded jacket and his Action Man crash helmet. He looked like a disturbing combination of Chris Hoy and the Michelin Man.

Husband and I had already agreed in a democratic and mature fashion who was to be Evel's assistant. 'If you don't do it, I'm cancelling Sky Sports.' I could have barbequed our dinner on the sparks off his heels.

'Right, I'm ready,' Cal announced, Batman trainers flashing

with glee. And off they went, three times round the netball court at breakneck speed. Husband was holding the back of the saddle, but I'm not sure whether he was providing added stability or clinging on for dear life.

'Let me go, Dad, let me go!' Low junior screamed with excitement.

Dad did as he was told.

Crash, bang, and then the screaming started – all of it coming from the direction of husband who had somehow managed to trip over his own feet and was sprawled out in the goal circle. Cal got up, dusted himself off, repositioned his crash helmet and climbed back on.

Husband wobbled back over to my viewing position on the packed-lunch bench.

'Your turn,' he announced, 'hamstring's pulled.' Ah, the old football injury. The one that usually rears its leg in times of shopping trips, wallpapering and anything to do with a lawnmower.

I had two choices: step up to the skid mark or let Cal go it alone. Only the fact that I knew there was nothing more than ten Winnie the Pooh plasters and a bottle of TCP in the first aid kit spurred me into action. Must remember to stock up on leg splints, crutches and a mobile stretcher.

Off I shot like an Exocet missile. Or, at least, what an Exocet missile would look like if it were bent double, terrified and flying in circles. Round we went until that joyous moment when I released him and he streaked away from me.

I watched him go, tears prickling my eyes.

'Okay, you can straighten up now,' husband declared, peeved that I'd been the one to achieve success in our son's latest milestone.

'Can't. Back's gone. That's why I'm crying.'

Five days later, my osteopath is fifty quid richer, and he's touting for even more business. 'You know, you really need to get out and exercise,' he announced over the noise of my cracking spine. 'Have you ever thought about cycling…?' ◆

Happy Birthday
to You...

First there was breastfeeding. Ever bashful, it took me a moment to come to terms with getting the bosoms out in public, but I did it.

Then there was the first time I was the parent-helper in my son's playgroup. Sixteen toddlers ganged up on me for putting out the wrong kind of biscuits and I was reduced to a snivelling wreck, rocking back and forward, clutching a packet of custard creams. But I survived. Just.

And what about the first long-haul flight with two toddlers? 'Ladies and gentlemen, on disembarking, please check the overhead lockers, remove all your belongings and collect your therapy vouchers from the air hostess on the way past.' I recovered eventually, although the fear of bored toddlers in a confined space hasn't quite left me yet.

Now, it's time for parenting test number 456: the birthday party.

As the whole playgroup/biscuit incident showed, much as I love kids, I get nervous around any more than four at a time. And that slides to two if there have been E-numbers involved. Look, it doesn't make me a bad person, just one with a low tolerance to chaos and the demands of small people who cry a lot.

Thus, my poor boys have never had a birthday shindig.

'Mum, can I have a party, please?'

'In two years' time when you start school.'

'Mum, can I have a party, please?'

'Next year when you start school.'

This year: 'Mum, can I have a party, please?'

'Next year when... Aaaaaargh! Where did that school uniform come from?'

There's no getting out of it – we're having a party.

Out came the clipboard and I put on my most efficient head – the one that usually only surfaces at times of financial discussions and when I'm pretending to car mechanics that I know what they're talking about.

I asked Low the Elder who he wanted to invite. Two hours later he was still talking. Forty-seven kids! Why couldn't I have given birth to a child who was shy, introverted and happy with his own company?

I knew I had to reduce the list but – ouch – a sore spot and a mortally embarrassing admission. One day last year, when he was still at nursery, he came home with his bottom lip hitting his boots. One of his 'best' pals was having a party and he hadn't been invited. The wee soul was distraught and my heart ached for him. Now, as parents, we have to take the mature ground and handle these situations in a responsible, sensitive and intelligent manner. So I did. I took to drawing the mother really evil looks behind her back and made effigies of her out of Play-Doh.

So, back to the guest list, how could I cut anyone out and risk inflicting that kind of trauma on a wee person, not to mention his/her mother? And, let's face it, an effigy of me would take up a whole lot of Play-Doh.

After an hour of ferocious debate that would have had an FBI negotiator reaching for the antiperspirant, I managed to get it down to forty by crossing off children I definitely didn't think would make it. Much as his pals in Galway love him, I think a trip across the Irish Sea for a box of chicken nuggets and two hours in a plastic play area might be a stretch.

Next the venue. I hit the phones like a double-glazing salesman. After the first three calls, I started to panic. Apparently, I had more chance of getting Robbie Williams to dress up as a Brewster Bear and sing 'Happy Birthday' backwards than I did of finding somewhere to hold a party for forty in three weeks' time.

More frantic calls, and just as son was about to get on the hotline to social services to complain about my substandard parenting, I finally found an available slot. Glee!

Then they told me the cost. It was difficult to talk further because I was hyperventilating into a party bag.

But, still, my boy is delighted and can't wait to see all his chums. Meanwhile, all I need to do now is buy the invitations, write them out, deliver them, make up goody bags, buy a cake, find a present and spend the next three weeks fretting that I've upset a five-year-old by forgetting to invite him.

Oh for those halcyon days of breastfeeding, playgroup and long-haul flights. ◆

Oh, For Flick's Sake

'**Welcome to the cinema** box office hotline. Please press one to hear showing times, two to book tickets and three to be subjected to such rubbish service that you'll begin to wish Will Smith hadn't bothered saving the earth in every movie he's ever been in.'

Now, you know it's not often that I have a moan. Oh, okay so it's every week, but that's only because Paris Hilton and several of our prominent MPs were put on this earth to make sure my hackles remain in an upright position at all times. This week, however, I've seriously got the hump, so I'm requesting permission to rant, rave and generally get more off my chest than Jordan would if her breast implants were stuck on with Velcro and readily detachable.

Maybe I'm missing something – like the gene that allows people to laugh off adversity, tribulation and really crap customer service – but next time I consider going to the cinema, remind me to do something far more pleasurable instead. Perhaps a colonic irrigation.

I usually love going to the flicks with my wee guys. Apart from the twenty-six trips to the toilet during the main feature, it's two hours of relative calm, when I don't have to worry about them doing karate or drawing on my couch.

I was rapt with excitement as I planned last Saturday's expedition to see *Wallace and Gromit*.

Step number one: phone the ticket line and pre-book the tickets; a fantastic concept that eliminates the need to stand in a ticket queue.

I called the automated hotline and the machine on the other end informed me that it used speech recognition technology. Oooer, very flash – a phone that understands what I'm saying. I've been married for over a decade and husband's yet to manage that.

A chipper voice ordered me to state the name of the cinema I wanted to visit. I responded loud and clear, in my very best voice.

'Did you say Landududnoaberystwyth?' it asked.

Not unless I've consumed a bottle of Lambrusco and developed an alcohol-related speech impediment. In the end, I gave up and I opted for the push-button service. Fifteen minutes later I got off the phone with three booked tickets and a stress-induced migraine.

We got to the cinema five minutes early and headed for the automatic ticket box. Credit card in – tickets out. At least that was the theory. In reality, a big sign saying 'Sorry, this machine is out of order' flashed across the screen.

We galloped over to the one at the other end of the foyer. Credit card in… 'Sorry, this machine is out of order.' Aaargh!

I looked around at the ticket desk. Shut. Never mind, there was one at the other side of the foyer. Back we gallop, every step and puff confirming that Liz McColgan and I are of a different species.

Of course, the cinema management had taken into account that both automatic ticket dispensers were broken by putting on extra staff. Yes, there were a whole two behind the desk. And you couldn't have got a longer queue if you'd been giving out free lapdances at a stag night. Don't ask me how I know that.

Twenty minutes later, we finally got our tickets.

'Mum, can I have a hot dog, please?' Low the Elder asked. 'Sorry pet, no time!' as we charged past yet another huge big line.

'I need the toilet!' Low the Younger wailed. We stormed the ladies, only to discover there was no loo roll in any of the manky cubicles. 'Baby' and 'Wipe' weren't the only four letter words that were muttered as I dived into my bag for my own supplies.

Panic was rising as I tucked one boy under each arm and rushed into the screening hall. We crept like prowlers down the aisle, climbed over twelve people and finally settled ourselves in the middle of the third row. And joy, the adverts were still showing so we hadn't missed the start of the movie.

I took a deep breath of soothing calm. We'd made it!

Unfortunately, so had the three six-foot-four guys that slid into the row in front of us, making my two wee blokes think there'd been an eclipse.

We clambered out of our row and down to the front, just as the movie was starting. There, in glorious Technicolor, at last, for our enjoyment, was... *Nanny McPhee*.

Yep, we were in the wrong hall.

Never again. Ever.

Instead, I'm going to concentrate on less stressful uses of my free time.

Anyone know the telephone number for the national colonic irrigation booking hotline? ◆

Because I Said So

'Mum, can I have a Gameboy for my birthday, please?' asked Low the Elder a couple of weeks before he reached the monumental age of five.

'No, honey.'

Bottom lip on floor. 'But why?'

'Because it'll turn you into an antisocial recluse who will confine himself to his room, subsist on a diet of Quavers and lose social skills and all powers of communication. This will then result in the inevitable degeneration into a life of crime and destitution that will end only when you're old, decrepit and alone, with thumbs the size of marrows.'

At least, that's what I meant. In reality, I invoked the first response from the Parental Code of Democracy, Fairness and Logic.

'Because I said so,' I replied.

'But, please,' he wailed.

Time for the second response from the Parental Code of

Democracy, Fairness and Logic – when under siege, take a deep breath, consider the options in an informed, intelligent manner... then panic and call in the cavalry.

'Go ask your dad.'

Five minutes later, back comes wee hopeful face, big eyes, fingers crossed. 'Dad says it's up to you.'

The cavalry had obviously invoked the third response – the one that involves shamelessly passing the buck during watching of sport on the telly or when the question is in any way related to the reproductive process of the human race.

'I'll think about it, pet,' I replied. Twenty seconds later I realised that he was still standing there. 'What is it?' I asked, puzzled by the Duracell Bunny's longest ever stationary period. 'I'm waiting until you've thought about it. So can I have one then?'

You've got to admire tenacity.

'Please, Mum, all my pals have got them and they're awesome!'

Awesome. Not even five yet and already he's talking like a bit-actor in *Baywatch*, while demonstrating the first ever instance of being swayed by peer pressure. Nooooo! That isn't supposed to happen yet. I thought peer pressure started somewhere around puberty and involved shoplifting, girls, or a sly cig behind a shed.

'So can I, Mum, can I, please?' snapped me out of my reverie.

Sigh. I want them to paint. I want them to play football

from dawn until dusk. I want them to have long, informed debates about important issues like the deterioration of the ozone layer, global warming and whether Bob the Builder could whoop Postman Pat in a square go. I don't want them to be sitting in a corner with a best pal called Super Mario.

But there's no escaping the fact that these things are part of modern-day culture and, I pondered, surely as long as I rationed the use of it, then it couldn't do any harm? Besides, if memory serves me right, Dr Robert Winston, world-renowned fertility expert and hirsute chappie from the BBC series *Child of Our Time*, concluded after extensive research that (in moderation) computer games improved kids' hand-to-eye co-ordination and brain reaction times. Och, it must be fine then. I'd trust that man with my fallopian tubes, so surely his advice on all things child-rearing must be sound.

So I admit it, I caved, and when the brand new five-year-old opened his new gadget on his birthday last Friday his grin could have steered ships away from reefs and rocks.

I, however, was still in turmoil. Buying him a Gameboy instead of something more outdoorsy and practical caused a momentary resurgence of the parental guilt hormone. The same one that made me start up a fund to pay for the counselling sessions they'll need when they're forty-five, have a midlife crisis and it's all blamed on the fact that their mother worked when they were children.

Anyway, I needn't have worried. Sunday afternoon, he appeared in full football kit and announced he was going into the back garden for a kick-about. Yay! He hasn't been completely overtaken by the cult of marrow thumbs.

'Not playing with your new game then?' asked I.

'Can't. Dad's playing with it and he won't give it back to me.'

It may be slow. It may be unreliable. But it's great to see that in times of trouble, strife and Gameboy guilt, the cavalry gets there eventually. ◆

On The Third Day
of Christmas...

On the third day of Christmas my true love gave to me...
stress, interludes of panic, and an overwhelming urge to tell
Santa where to stick his ho, ho, ho's.

Actually, none of these things have been caused by my true
love, but since he is the 'blame default setting' for everything
that goes wrong in this house, he's being made to suffer.

To be honest (and I reserve the right to deny this
admission when it suits), this week's mayhem is all down to
unforeseen circumstances and the fact that I could have Janet
Street Porter's dental superiority and I'd still have bitten off
more than I could chew.

And it's all the more perplexing because I was sure I was
organised. Obviously, however, I missed chapter 327 of *The
Mothering Manual* – the one entitled: 'In the Run-up to
Christmas Your Children Will Suddenly Adopt the Social
Life of a Magaluf tour rep.'

On The Third Day of Christmas...

I'm no longer just a mother; I'm now my two boys'
Entertainment Co-ordinator. My three-year-old has been
to more parties in the last week than I've been to in a year.
He now thinks Santa is his new best friend and will be gutted
if the fat bloke in the red suit doesn't start popping round
one night a week for a play date. My five-year-old's schedule
is even more frantic. This is his first year in school so he has
a packed programme of nativity plays, carol services, parties
and Christmas lunches. And each event sees me running
around like a headless turkey organising the appropriate
clothes, food and presents, while answering questions about
the logic of our Christmas traditions – like why does Santa
use reindeers when helicopters would be far more efficient?

Still, at least things aren't too pressured work-wise at the
moment. It's not as if it's only nine days, three hours and
forty-two minutes until my next book is due to be delivered
to my publisher's office. Hear that thudding noise? That's
the sound of me hitting the floor in a panic-induced faint.
Nine days, at least two of which will be written off due to
the medical condition chocmintos toxicosis – the inability
to move from the couch due to chronic abuse of After Eights.

I could weep. Actually, I did on Sunday, when one of my
hands got jammed in the garage door. Cue big bandage. Oh,
yes, it never rains but it snows. Nine days to finish the book
and I'm down to one hand – meaning my normal two-finger
typing output has been reduced to a single digit.

Present wrapping has also been transformed from a fun,

yuletide task into a feat of one-handed contortion. And last-minute festive gift buying will necessitate asking shop assistants to tie things to my back.

Incidentally, on the subject of shopping, I had all my gifts in by the end of November. Then I got to Chapter 328 of *The Mothering Manual*: Small Children Change Their Minds About What They Want for Christmas on a Daily Basis. Santa would need to have multiple personality disorder to deal with the wishes of my wee elves. Yesterday: a Power Rangers' suit, an Action Man and Robin Hood's castle. Today: a Batman bike, a skateboard and a pet reindeer. In the last month I've spent more time at the Toys R Us returns desk than the people who work there.

I'm just keeping my sore fingers crossed that all the mayhem subsides and I get back to ambidextrous living by Christmas Day. We're planning a solemn, peaceful occasion – right up until fourteen people show up for lunch. Fourteen. People. Christmas. Lunch. Sorry, I had to repeat that because I'm still in denial. I am the woman for whom cordon bleu cooking involves a sandwich toaster. I hate food preparation with a passion normally reserved for expense-cheating politicians and anything containing cranberries.

So a wee message to my one true love – forget the partridge in the pear tree. On the first day of Christmas I'd like a new bandage, a secretary, a personal shopper, two happy wee boys and the entire staff of our local Chinese restaurant. And if Santa's a bit pushed, just get him to bring it all by helicopter. ◆

2006

Battling Brothers and Earth Mothers ››››

Oh, Brother!

Oh, Brother!

Not many people are aware that Russell Crowe and I have something in common. Oh, yes, two peas in a pod.

Well, almost.

Obviously I'm not Australian, male or prone to developing outbreaks of facial hair. Not since I discovered epilation.

Sadly, we don't share acting talent. Or Oscars. Or a multi-millionaire jet-set lifestyle. And, much as I have been known to occasionally get frazzled with inefficient hotel workers, I've so far refrained from any situation involving alleged violence, a receptionist, and the latest weapon from Binatone.

Furthermore, as far as I know, Russ doesn't spend his Saturday afternoons in Evans' changing rooms repeating the words 'effing, effing, effing', while trying to manoeuvre his bod into a size sixteen summer frock.

But Russ (I feel I can call him that – as long as he's out of earshot, obviously) and I are both… oh the suspense… a parent of two wee boys. Or at least he soon will be, according to his announcement this week that his wife Danielle is expecting their second son this summer.

So, never one to miss a chance to ingratiate myself with someone who has holiday homes in exotic places (credit cards are maxed out – I'm desperate), I thought I'd share the benefits of my maternal wisdom by passing on some cerebral, spiritual little nuggets of my experiences of raising brothers.

First of all, it has to be said that the inherent bond between brothers who are close in age is a beautiful thing. My sons are five and four, and their frequent demonstrations of reciprocal love, their natural instincts to defend each other, and their lively interactions can often bring a tear to the eye. Especially when a Batman car hurled at speed catches you right on the shins.

I've also learned that brothers can have the same gene pool, environment and upbringing and they can still be polar opposites, with different preferences when it comes to food (result: preparation of two different meals every night), pastimes (sports fanatic/couch potato) and toys. Although that last rule of thumb is defunct if there is only one of said toy, in which case they will both want it and a fight to the death will ensue. When this happens, a firm rule of owner/possession must be applied – except if altercation occurs in a public place, when whoever screams the loudest gets what they want. It's the law.

Brothers have a driving need to establish their own identity, often using tactics that disassociate them from their sibling, e.g. name-changing. As a result, I am not currently the mother of the Low brothers, but my sons Dr Doom and SpongeBob SquarePants are doing just fine.

As a nation, we have many paranormal occurrences: crop circles, UFO sightings, Derek Acorah's hair. In homes with two small boys, there is the spooky and inexplicable phenomenon of the phantom crayon – a manifestation that normally targets soft furnishings and anything in your wardrobe that's white.

They will disagree on everything, except the comic merits of passing wind, pants and the word 'pump'.

They can be too tired to remember their manners, tidy their rooms or brush their teeth, but they'll still have enough energy to play football or swing from the curtains while making Tarzan noises.

They are programmed with a voice system capable of repeating, 'Muuuum, he's annoying me,' until the end of time.

Like teenage girls, they have a strange compulsion to visit toilets en masse. I won't go into details of their other bathroom idiosyncrasies, other than to say that, as the parent of brothers, you will never again sit down on a toilet seat without checking it first. And when you hear, 'Whoo-hoo, mine's hitting the ceiling,' you will immediately understand and head for B&Q.

And a word of warning… When rearing boys, it's probably best not to ponder their historical role models: the Krays, the Gallaghers, the Mitchells or worse, the evil duo who have

caused excruciating pain and misery to the ears of millions –
the Chuckle Brothers.

Although it's probably safe to say that, with the state of
the British dental care system, it's unlikely that they'll ever
become the Osmonds.

So, Russ, here endeth the lesson. And if you want to
experience my boys in action, we're available for trips
to sunny holiday homes. Preferably the sooner the better –
before that new Evans' summer frock gets crayon on it. ◆

Morning Has Broken... Me!

Reasons I'll never pass my HMC (Higher Maternal Competence) in Parenthood, number 2,342 – mornings. The very thought of them makes me want to lie down in a dark room until the *Neighbours* theme tune signals that it's lunchtime.

Ladies, is it just me? Is mine the only household in the world where mornings are an exercise in urban warfare?

Back in my teens, I occasionally envisioned what my happy little family life of the future would look like. We'd all sit around the breakfast table: I'd be a size 10 and look like the blonde one in Bananarama and my husband, Morten Harket, the mullet-topped lead singer of A-ha, would gaze adoringly at our two little bilingual child prodigies.

Later, in my PE days (Pre-Episiotomy – blokes, ask the wife and have your best sympathetic face ready), mornings were a hassle-free operation consisting of a quick shower, a coffee, a ciggie and a 100-metre dash to the car.

Now? I adore my boys, but mornings are chaotic mayhem, with a noise level that warrants an ASBO.

I try to be a serene earth mother, but instead I end up getting louder and louder until someone either answers me or throws something at me in the hope of breaking my voice box.

Low the Elder usually climbs into our bed some time before dawn, where he proceeds to sleep like a starfish, leaving husband and I three inches of mattress each. He then wakes up at the first claxon of the alarm clock and requests sustenance. He's five, so he hasn't quite sussed out yet that repetition isn't necessarily a good thing.

'Can we go down for breakfast now Mum, can we, can we, can we, CAN WE?'

Meanwhile, I'm still trying to prise open my eyes and remember my name.

Eventually, I give in and allow myself to be dragged into the bedroom of Low the Younger, who is four but thinks he's a fully-fledged teenager who should be allowed to lie in bed until he's old enough to shave.

'Come on honey, time to get up,' I whisper lovingly.

He throws the duvet over his head and informs everyone living within our postcode area that he's 'STILL TIRED!!!!!!'

Twenty minutes of negotiation, bribery and coercion later, we get to the kitchen table – one still repeating the breakfast mantra and the other threatening to leave home.

When I was in Bananarama, our disciplined, perfect family

all feasted on the same breakfast. Yeah, right. That would be a Frostie too far for my lot, who each require their own individually designed assortment of Jamie Oliver-approved edibles.

'I'm not hungry,' declares son number one, the very same child who has been pulling me towards the kitchen since daybreak. Hear that banging noise? That's my head coming into contact with the cereal cupboard.

Next comes the ablutions bit. Otherwise known as 'chasing two wee boys around the house clutching two toothbrushes and a tube of Colgate'. Closely followed by another circuit of the house with a face sponge and soap, and loud yells from me demanding that they stop playing football in the house or I'll confiscate the goalposts: an Ikea lamp and the ironing board.

Then comes the Pants Scrum of Death. 'I'm wearing the Batman ones!'

'No, they're MINE!'

'Muuuuuuuuuuuum!!!'

At which point, the clock has jumped forward thirty minutes and we're now in danger of being late. Nooooo! Panic!

Their uniform/clothes get thrust on, only for them both to take another drink of juice and spill it down their front, necessitating a repeat of the whole exercise.

Then I remember I haven't made up the packed lunches, checked homework, made the beds and I'm still in my pyjamas.

Oh, and son number one still hasn't eaten his breakie.

I somehow manage to get them sorted and in the car, deposit son two at nursery and flee to his brother's school, just in time for noise of the bell to drown out the noise coming from my thumping heart.

Phew. Made it. And as I look down at that gorgeous little face, still stuffing the last of his breakfast into his mouth as he leans over to say goodbye, I realise that I've managed to conquer another morning. I did it! And survived!

'Mum, did I tell you we're to bring in cakes today?' ◆

Lilo Lil

It's that time again... Husband is giving me that wide berth normally reserved for danger-fraught circumstances like deadlines, contagious illness and PMT. I cracked two toes on the empty suitcase that's been lying in the hall for days waiting to be put in to service. The passports that have been in plain sight for months have now gone missing – especially worrying as it coincides with the disappearance of a black marker pen and the arrival of a suspiciously guilty look on my four-year-old's face. And I'm wondering if there's a safe, non-surgical way to lose four stone by the weekend.

I'd give a heartfelt, howling rendition of 'Summertime Blues', but this time of the year is up there with Christmas on the 'Great Excuse For Martyrdom' scale, so I've taken to stomping around, while sighing pointedly and playing keepy-uppy with my petted lip instead.

'Chill out,' says husband. From a safe distance and with the added protection of a riot shield and safety goggles. Chill out? Chill out?

I'm a martyr on a schedule; I haven't got bloody time to chill out.

And I'm not the only one who's suffering from pre-holiday stress. Whenever I enter the room, the kids now adopt a look of panicked terror and check out the emergency exits.

But then, they know if they want to get as far as sun, sea and laughing at their mother trying to successfully mount a lilo, then they have to get past the most tortuous event of their year: the holiday haircut.

Why do small boys hate anyone touching their hair? Why can they not sit at peace for more than ten minutes? Why do I think that a Saturday job in a hairdressing salon when I was fourteen has somehow given me the kind of skills you'd expect from Vidal Sassoon?

And why did I only ever learn one haircut? Since I've appointed myself responsible for the crowning glories of our whole family, we all march into the airport looking like fully paid-up members of the Tufty Club.

At least everything that will happen between now and the check-in desk is comfortingly predictable.

We leave approximately forty-eight hours from now, so that gives loads of time to pack up our capsule wardrobe, then re-pack it when we discover that the collective weight of our cases is roughly the same as a 747.

Then we'll find the documentation for our annual travel insurance policy – that expires an hour before we leave.

We'll discover that we've forgotten to collect our foreign currency five minutes after the Post Office has shut.

We'll remember to book the taxi – and discover that we won't all fit in one cab.

We'll make a point of putting the camera in a safe, secure section of the luggage. Fourteen photo-free days later, we'll come home to mysteriously find it in its usual place in the kitchen cupboard.

We'll pack the entire stock of the Early Learning Centre, Toys R Us and the Argos catalogue for the children's amusement on the plane. They'll be saying they're bored before the wheels leave the runway.

We'll find last year's suntan lotion… has leaked all over our newly packed clothing.

We'll cancel the papers, ask a neighbour to put out the bins, clear the fridge of perishables, beg a nice friend to cut the grass, stop the mail, pay all outstanding bills, clean the house, stock up the first aid kit and change the beds.

Sorry, just realised that through the whole of that last bit I was using the term 'we'. I do, of course, mean 'little old martyr me'.

Husband will show up half an hour before we leave with four pairs of kecks, a pair of flip-flops, a book and his swimmies. And somehow he'll still have something to wear every night of the two-week break. Woe.

Because I Said So

Thankfully, preparing for a holiday is like childbirth – the minute it ends and you reap the rewards, ecstasy kicks in and you forget the pain…

At least until next year's countdown to Tufty Tours. ◆

Power Cut

What do you get if you mix the lethal combination of Lambrusco, Internet travel websites and a new credit card? Two weeks in Florida and a bank manager who calls security at the mention of your name.

But, oh the excitement! We were all set for a fortnight of family bliss, relaxation and sun, sun, sun… I know, I know, don't even say it. My predictions are notoriously inaccurate. This is why I've never won the lottery, swore Madonna would be a one-hit wonder and was convinced that the Bay City Rollers would outlast the Rolling Stones.

However, day two and not even torrential rain could dampen our spirits as we headed to the fantastic Disney MGM Studios, home of Indiana Jones, the Muppets and many grown adults dressed as animals – something that's probably outlawed in several conservative US states.

After a couple of hours wandering around in our undeniably chic (!) waterproof ponchos we came across hoards of people waiting for, drum roll, the Power Rangers. My heart sank. The Power Rangers are now strictly banned in this house. Ditto Star Wars, Pokemon, Jackie Chan, Teen Titans and anything else that has scenes of karate, shooting, fighting or general random assault.

I have two wee boys – at the merest suggestion of violence in a television programme, they immediately commandeer the Dyson and the pole that opens the loft hatch, brandish them at each other in a playful yet threatening manner, and before you can say 'Accident & Emergency' I'm digging out the first aid kit and dishing out the detention. Someone once gave my five-year-old a Power Rangers DVD – after one viewing he declared a planetary war on his wee brother and attempted a triple-back somersault from halfway up the stairs. Said DVD now resides under the couch, and will not be retrieved until he's old enough to view it without morphing into Tartan Power Ranger – the one whose mother runs around behind him shouting, 'Stop that kung fu nonsense right now or I'm burying the biscuit tin in the garden.'

Back to Disney. Regardless of my superhero embargo, my boys were ecstatic when a huge open-top car appeared, blaring the Power Rangers theme tune, and off jumped five dodgy looking characters in luminous helmets and jumpsuits so tight you could've counted the intergalactic change in their pockets. One look at my two wee heroes' rapturous faces and, despite my disapproval, I knew we had to join the huge queue waiting for a photo opportunity. Twenty minutes later, we were next in line to meet one of the Rangers. A few more moments, a few steps forward and… 'Sorry guys, the Power Rangers have to get back to their vehicle now,' an official informed us as they suddenly bolted back to their vehicle and took off. Apparently there was a universe that needed saving. Or it was nearly closing time in the Disney staff canteen.

Cue two wee trembling lips. Actually, three if you count mine, but I maintain that was due to a chill caused by rain-soaked nethers. There was nothing else for it – we had to stay in the park for almost three more hours, waiting for their next appearance.

Three long, wet, impatient hours.

When they finally did reappear, there was an undignified, mad scrummage back to the front of the photograph queue. Until husband pulled me back and told me to behave myself.

Call it temporary insanity, but at that moment there was nothing in the world more important than a Kodak moment with a bloke dressed like an Eighties throwback. We shuffled back up the queue. Almost there. Almost. Nearly. It was just about our turn when the heavens opened and we were subjected to another downpour. Immediately, I realised with horror what was about to happen. The rain-fearing Ranger nearest to us quickly turned, searched out his car, started towards it and… was met with a mad Scotswoman blocking his path, saying, 'You'll have time for one more photo, Mr Power Ranger' in a voice that made it clear that rejection was not an option.

Yep, the Power Rangers may have defended our galaxy, conquered enemies from the outer cosmos and saved the earth on a weekly basis, but one of them almost got his Lycra pinged by a jet-lagged, soaking wet, PMT-crazed Glaswegian mother in a plastic poncho.

On reflection, I'm mortified but, hey, it was worth it. Two delighted boys, great memories and fabulous photos on their bedroom walls.

I just wish I could find the Dyson and the pole for the loft hatch. ◆

Boy Oh Boy...

The most common conversation I had when I was pregnant for the second time began something along the lines of, 'Aw, congratulations! And you've a wee boy already – bet you're hoping for a girl this time.'

Actually, that's a lie. With permanent morning sickness, the manoeuvrability of a Portakabin and a new familiarity with creams that go in places nothing should ever go, the most common conversation included the words 'never again', 'celibacy' and 'snip'.

But back to the girl thing. In truth, after six years of fertility treatment that included hormone treatments, count-less medical procedures and more mood swings than a temperamental pendulum, I was just thrilled that I'd somehow managed to defy my dodgy ovaries and have one child and another on the way. I would have been equally grateful, thrilled and excited whether I had a boy or a girl.

But I have to admit, another wee guy was a gorgeous, not

to mention pragmatic, prospect. I already had all the blue stuff and knew all the words to the *Spiderman* theme tune. And, let's face it, throughout history there have been many examples of the unbreakable bonds and great things achieved by brothers: the Wright brothers invented the aeroplane, the Grimm brothers became legends in the literary world, and, most significantly of all, the Kemp brothers sang 'True', and that's the best snogging song ever recorded.

So when one of my girlfriends announced this week that she's having her second boy, I was thrilled for her and more than happy to pass on the nuggets of wisdom I've picked up over the last five years as mother of two small men. It's been a profound experience that has helped me grow as a person and reach a whole new level of karmic spirituality, as demonstrated by the fact that I can now name all of Bob the Builder's crew and list the top-ten threats to the galaxy in alphabetical order.

Things that having two boys has taught me:

1. There are 2,654 uses in the English language of the word 'pump'. All of them side-splittingly hilarious to males under four feet tall.
2. I am destined to sit on a wet toilet seat for the rest of my life.
3. Farting is not a bodily function, it's a form of entertainment surpassed only by surreptitious nose picking and anything to do with mud.

4. The best time to announce that you've learned a new swear word is in a crowded shop. Ditto asking mum to explain words relating to bodily functions or body parts.

5. Sniffing should be an Olympic sport.

6. As should burping, giggling and projectile peeing.

7. At the end of every day, boys slump into exhaustion – until you mention the word 'bed'. This is the trigger for an energy surge strong enough to fuel a new world record for complaining.

8. It's never too wet, too windy, too cold, too snowy or too late for a footie kick-about in the back garden.

9. The fashion must-have is anything dirty, mucky or torn at the knees – preferably within five minutes of putting it on.

10. It is compulsory to acquire food stains and suspicious damp patches on the way to visit relatives.

11. Felt pen is permanent even when it's not supposed to be.

12. Brussels sprouts are handpicked from Satan's garden.

13. You should never leave home without your Star Wars pants.

14. Scented candles can provide momentary relief; they cannot, however, perform miracles.

15. There are three standard replies to all accusatory questions: 'It wasn't me,' 'I wasn't there' and 'He did it.'

16. Words of complaint, annoyance or indignation should always have at least six vowels. Aaaaaaw Muuuuuum!

17. Nothing, but *nothing*, swells the heart like two gorgeous wee guys showering you with kisses and vowing that they'll never leave their mum. Although I do realise that the effect of this may change when said guys reach middle age.

Profound. Deep. Spiritual.

Yep, spawning brothers has been a true blessing. And I can only hope that throughout their lives the boys draw on each other's support to achieve all the things that would make their mother proud: successful careers, healthy relationships, and writing the best snogging song ever recorded. ◆

Away With the Fairies

'Mum, Mum, another tooth fell out today and I didn't even cry,' screeched five-year-old Low the Elder, in a voice so high-pitched with excitement that neighbourhood dogs added earmuffs to their Christmas list.

'Fabulous,' says me, full of parental emotion, 'so you know what that means, don't you?'

The answers I was going for were:

a. he's getting to be a big boy now;
b. he was so, so brave not to shed a tear; or
c. his big tooth would soon come through.

The answer I got? A huge toothless grin, followed by, 'Yep, four packets of football stickers and three Curly Wurlies.'

The gum was still throbbing, the tooth was still warm, yet he'd already divvied up his dosh from the Tooth Fairy. Oh, he makes me so proud. I swear that boy is going to be an economist when he grows up.

Or treasurer of his cell block's savings scheme.

However, according to new research, I should enjoy his innocent optimism while I can because apparently childhood is on the way out. A survey by TV channel, the Cartoon Network, has concluded that today's kids stop believing in characters like the Tooth Fairy, elves and Santa a whole four years earlier than their parents' generation.

Which means my boys will stop writing letters to Lapland at the devastatingly young age of thirty-six.

Apparently, back in the good old days, when taking drugs meant Disprin and the worldwide web was what Spiderman used to catch the bad guys, sixty-seven per cent of adults still believed in fairies at the age of ten. Now? Tinkerbell is up the dole office looking for her giro shortly after a kid's sixth birthday.

But the biggest tragedy of the new findings, and yes, I am aware that this makes me sound like a nostalgic old fart, is that the survey confirmed that games from our childhood are nothing but a distant memory.

Although, I suppose in today's consumerist nanny state of cosseted kids and rampant political correctness, it's not really surprising.

Peevers (posh name: hopscotch) now results in an ASBO for chalking up pavements. Health & Safety would batter you to death with a pair of clackers for building a rope swing. And E-numbers rule out standing still long enough for a game of statues.

Away With the Fairies

Today's extended families mean that a game of aunts and uncles would take so long it would have to be interrupted by life-sustaining acts like eating and sleeping.

Bicycle helmets are a great idea that I fully endorse, support, and force my boys to wear. However, there's no denying that they've replaced the pure gallus headgear that was mandatory for riding our Choppers – the hood of an anorak, with said jacket flying in the wind behind us like a cape, à la Batman/ Wonder Woman/Elvis in the Las Vegas years.

And, of course, iPods, Playstations, Xboxes, Nintendos, computers, satellite TV and Gameboys have superseded our favourite playthings: pals.

Which is just as well, because role-playing is out of fashion, too. A game of doctors and nurses would undoubtedly now result in a lawsuit for medical misconduct. Cops and robbers would violate the perpetrator's human rights. And playing cowboys could lead to legal action for contraventions of the firearms code.

Modern technology means that it would now be insanity to snog your boyfriend behind the bicycle sheds – someone would film it on a mobile phone and your dad would have irrefutable photographic evidence within seconds.

And the birth of kids' designer labels has banished those heady days when there were only two types of trainers: plimsolls and Green Flash.

Nope, I wouldn't trade growing up in the Seventies and Eighties for anything, and I wish that someone, somewhere

– Santa, the Tooth Fairy, the nanny state – could deliver to today's children the really important things in life: innocence, freedom, and a childish, outdoor life full of friends and riotous fun.

Oh, and any chance that while they're at it they could throw in four packets of football stickers and three Curly Wurlies? ◆

2007

Milk Breaks and Saddle-aches ››››

Crazed By the Bell

There were tears. There was the occasional wail. There was even an embarrassing act of lamppost hugging, a delay tactic that was finally counteracted by peeling ten fingers off the metal pole and the promise of a medicinal Dairy Milk.

Oh, and Low the Younger was a wee bit apprehensive about his first visit to his new school, too.

It's Operation Primary One, minus sixty-two days and counting, and boy, Houston, do we have a problem.

I know it's pathetic, but I have to admit that the thought of waving my baby off through those gates for the first time is up there with back-to-back episodes of *Little House on the Prairie* on my sob-o-meter.

Two years ago we did the same induction tour with Low the Elder, or Darth Vader as he was then known – it was during his dalliance with the dark side when he changed his name and used the power of the force to projectile pee, suck up spaghetti and confiscate all his wee brother's toys.

Darthie is an extrovert; a confident, fearless wee thing who loves change, thrives on excitement and takes everything in his stride, so I didn't have a moment's hesitation about nudging him out of the nest and into the land of ABCs and miniature-sized WCs.

But his wee brother is a completely different kettle of fish fingers.

He's a sweet, naïve little soul who still believes that the flashing alarm sensor in the corner of the living room is 'Santa's camera'. He loves his bears. His favourite thing in the world (other than Alphabites, his Scalextric set and his SpongeBob SquarePants DVD) is having his face rubbed until he falls asleep. And he still thinks the only evil in the world (Darth Vader aside) comes in the form of Superman's enemies and is kept under control by wearing his pants over his trousers... just as long as there's time to take regular crime-fighting breaks for some milk, a banana and a wee nap before tea.

As we trudged towards his new classroom, he got slower and slower, biting his bottom lip while my heart filled with woe as I watched his shyness take over. By the time we got to the door, he'd surgically attached himself to the back of my jumper.

My dread rose in direct proportion to my thumping heart-beat as the uncertainties raced through my mind. Would he cry? Would he flee? Would he spend the rest of his life with his face immersed in my favourite fluffy jumper?

Would snot come out of mohair with just a gentle wash at thirty degrees?

And that's when it happened. HNC (Has No Clue) in Parenthood, Module 346 – Just When You Think You Know Your Child Inside Out, He'll Prove You Completely Wrong.

The minute we crossed the classroom threshold, he peeked out from behind his maternal camouflage, grinned from ear to ear then bounded over to announce his arrival to a gathering of fellow newbies in the corner. He confidently introduced himself. He sang songs. He quickly acquired a name badge, eleven new pals and a school baseball cap that he insists on wearing backwards.

He had such a blast that over an hour later we had to invoke the sacred parental act of persuasion ('If you don't come right now you'll miss the beginning of *Scooby Doo*') to get him to leave.

So, of course, I'm now feeling relieved, confident and full of enthusiasm for the start of this new stage in his life. Okay, I'm lying – on the dread scale it still sits somewhere between the dentist and the annual gynaecological thing that makes your eyes water.

But at least I'm not alone. Having consulted several other parents, I've been reliably informed that the separation anxiety that mothers feel when their youngest child takes their first steps towards independence takes a while to subside. By their reckoning, I should be fine by the time he starts shaving.

Because I Said So

In the meantime, I've got sixty-two days to psyche myself up, accept the situation and prepare myself for the inevitable... and stock up on those medicinal bars of Dairy Milk. ❖

Howdy Pardner

Well, howdy pardners! Ahm, a-walking like a cowboy, so ah thought ah'd talk like one, too.

No, I haven't taken up line dancing and got carried away with the whole Western theme. Although I did try that once – my granny dragged me there on the premise that 'loads of young ones go' (there were two people under sixty) and 'it'll keep you fit'. She overlooked the crucial fundamental error in that sentence, i.e. I wasn't fit in the first place. After half an hour I was sweating like a polar bear in Benidorm, and thoroughly mortified that a seventy-five-year-old woman in an embroidered waistcoat was twirling like a Latin American champion while shouting at me to 'keep up or move to the back'.

But the real reason for the increased sensitivity of the gluteus maximus and acutely painful quadriceps (translation: my arse is aching and my inner thighs feel like they've been cracking nuts) is down to something a bit more sporty.

It's all Low the Younger's fault. Since the moment he could talk – and despite never having been within a hundred yards of anything with udders – he's wanted to be a farmer. This is also the boy who has a cleaning fixation that compels him to do the dishes every night, mop the kitchen floor on an hourly basis, wear only spotlessly clean clothes and run the Dyson round the house 'just for fun'. Honestly, he could be the poster boy for Flash. Yet... he wants to spend the rest of his life in a job that requires daily contact with muck. I don't think he's thought this through.

Anyway, in keeping with my thought process that if he has a passion in life there's less chance of him hitting puberty and deciding to hang about the streets in a shell suit, smoking ciggies and developing a high-grade tonic wine habit, I've been trying to get him interested in a hobby. I went for the obvious ones first. Football? He looked at me like I'd just suggested Buzz Lightyear was an ineffective guardian of the universe. That would be a no, then. Same reaction with rugby, golf and athletics. Okay, I was getting the message that pastimes in the sweat/potential for injury sector were probably out.

Knitting? (Hey, I'm all for cross-gender activities that break down outdated stereotypes, further promote equality between the sexes and result in a natty new scarf.) Another resounding no.

'Well, what would you like to do then, honey?'

He thought about it for a second and then... 'Horses.'

'What?' My stomach dropped to the floor. In a family

where a love of betting on the gee-gees is in the DNA (but I swear I've finally cut up my William Hill account card), this was the last thing I wanted to hear. I had visions of Saturday afternoons at Hamilton races with Low junior shouting, 'Pocket money on number four, each way bet, and put the winnings on the outsider in the three o'clock.'

'I'd like to go horse riding,' he clarified. Phew.

So a-horse riding we went, and when we got there, I realised I had a choice – I could watch or I could indulge in an unfulfilled childhood longing and book a lesson for me too. And, anyway, as a seventy-five-year-old in an embroidered waistcoat should have said, it might even get me fit.

So I foolishly, *foolishly* joined in. I should have taken the hint when my horse was led from the stable, took one look at my rather big-boned frame, and asked for the number of the RSPCA.

The poor thing nearly buckled at the knees when I clambered on. Thankfully, I was too busy clinging on for dear life to worry. Thirty minutes of developing my 'rising trot' later (up, down, up, down, squeeze those legs), I felt like the horse had trotted over me.

And it's not just my posterior that's bruised. After the lesson, we debriefed my brother on our new hobby. 'So what was your horse called then?'

'Lucky,' replied my beaming wee boy.

'Guess what mine was called?' I demanded gleefully, desperate to take my mind off the pain by joining in the fun.

He looked me up and down, obviously contemplating common horse names while absorbing a mental picture of his sister on a steed.

'Er... Clydesdale?'

Ouch.

So what do I have to do to get my boy interested in knitting? ◆

It's a Mother of a Thing

Another week, another award slips through my unmanicured fingers. I'm devastated to announce that I did not – sob – make it on to the list of the nation's top five Yummy Mummies. I mean, what have Nigella Lawson, Myleene Klass, Angelina Jolie, Kate Winslet and Davina McCall got that I haven't? I'm utterly inconsolable and I just don't understand it. In fact, if I cry any more I'm going to get snot all over my shapeless fleece.

Okay, so maybe it's not such a newsflash.

The only real surprise about the survey results was that the Material Girl wasn't on there. Madonna? Definitely a top Yummy Mummy. She was even spotted last week, all glammed up, leaving an upmarket London hotel clutching a bag containing a sex aid. And no, I don't mean a can of Red Bull to keep her awake. She had one of those things that makes strange buzzing noises and gives you a beamer when it sets off the security alerts at airports.

Surely that kind of equipment is the true, true measure of a Yummy Mummy. A Slummy Mummy doesn't have the energy or the inclination, and she knows the chances of finding spare batteries are up there with the chances of locating her make-up bag without a search party and a compass.

I try to make time for a little spot of preening and pampering. I do. But somehow I'm one of those women who finds that running a house, two children under six and a full-time job puts me firmly in the grooming category labelled 'Dressed in the dark – washable fabrics only'.

I have no idea how the organised mums do it. It's like there's a secret race of Supermothers out there who have twenty-nine hours in the day, several assistants, and the ability to pause time while they reapply their lippy every fifteen minutes.

Everywhere I go, I see these tanned, lithe women with yoga mats under their arms, breezing past in co-ordinated outfits with a two-week-old baby strapped to their body. When my boys were two weeks old, I was still commando-crawling to the corner shop in the hope that no-one would spot that I was wearing a dressing gown, sporting two-inch roots and slippers in the shape of elephants that some comedian had bought me as a witty jibe at my pre-birth physique.

It's not that I don't have a thorough understanding of the criteria and the required standards of Superior Motherdom – I just don't seem to be able to attain the entry-level qualifications.

It's a Mother of a Thing

Yummy Mummies don't save their dry-clean-only clothes for weddings and funerals. They cook organic meals from scratch. They smell of Eau de Really Expensive. Their hair has never seen a split end and they have a house, a social schedule and a waxing regime that run to military precision.

My clothes are black and shapeless, alternated with black and shapeless, and if I'm feeling really daring I might go for something that's, er, black and shapeless. Mealtimes are punctuated by the ping of the microwave. There are hikers halfway up my ironing pile. I carry a faint whiff of Eau de Flash-for-Bathrooms. And my legs have applied for a lottery grant and official status as Scotland's national forest.

A Yummy Mummy's stomach muscles ping back like overstretched bungee ropes the minute she gives birth. I'm taking a far slower, steadier approach to losing the baby weight, and plan to do it before my youngest son's next birthday. His sixth.

I know I should disregard the whole Yummy Mummy ethos as a media-generated stereotype designed to make the more normal, exhausted, multitasking mother feel inferior, but the thing is, I want to be one of them. I've had five years of woeful mismanagement of my personal presentation standards and it's time for change. Yummy Mummies of the world, I'm coming to join you… just as soon as I can get a make-up bag, a beauty therapist, a yoga mat and twenty-nine hours in the day. ◆

I'm Dreaming of a...

Oh, it's so close I can almost visualize it. Our boys will gently rouse us awake, with a whispered, 'Good Morning, Mummy and Daddy'. The dulcet tones of Bing Crosby, crooning 'White Christmas' will waft through the house as we pad downstairs to see what Santa has left us. We'll open the presents, taking the time to wonder at every little trinket and toy. And then we'll bathe, dress and welcome the family, enjoy mid-morning drinkies and nibbles before the cook announces that lunch is ready. And what a banquet! We'll feast on the most tender of turkeys and the finest vegetables, enjoying the company before rounding off the day with a brisk, crisp afternoon walk and... Okay, okay, so I'm lying.

I reckon I almost got away with it until the 'brisk walk' bit. If I'm going to put one foot in front of the other for more than fifty consecutive metres, there would have to be shopping involved and a cappuccino and a foot spa at the end. It's not laziness – it's post-traumatic stress after the infamous 2004

I'm Dreaming of a...

Boxing Day stroll/long white fake-fur coat/head first in a muddy lane debacle that scarred me for life.

Alas, our Christmas morning might just play out a little differently from the fairy tale above.

The kids will bounce on our heads at 5.30 a.m., screaming in the national tongue of the Planet Helium, the duvet will be dragged off, one boy will grab each ankle and pull until I land with such a thud that the Met Office will register an earth tremor in Glasgow that measures approximately 2.4 on the Richter scale. And at least 10 on the mother's bruised buttocks scale.

We'll race down to the living room and either husband or I will suddenly realise that Santa has once again forgotten to eat his biscuits and Rudolph's tin of carrots remains unopened. Cue the need for an impromptu distraction – two verses and a chorus of 'Jingle Bells' usually does the trick – while said items are surreptitiously removed. The only exception to this annual oversight was the year we came down to a plate of crumbs – a scene that led to a devastating realisation and a phone call to Environmental Health to deal with the infestation of mice in our chimney.

The calming, spiritual strains of Noddy Holder screeching, 'It's Christmas!!!!!!' will add to the atmosphere, while we unwrap the presents in the manner of a plague of locusts devouring a cornfield. Then comes the most famous of our quaint family Christmas traditions – husband's annual strop because the garage/castle/fort requires a professional burglary team to remove it from the packaging and a consultation with NASA on how to put the 447 pieces together.

Drinkies and nibbles? Absolutely. An iced-top mince pie and a coffee from my swanky new coffee maker – the one I still haven't worked out how to use properly so everything comes out tasting like watered-down Bisto. Don't ask.

And we'll still be in our pyjamas, watching that triumph of classic filmmaking, *Monsters Inc.*, when the family start to arrive. I love my family. I do. But I have absolutely no idea why they subject themselves to Christmas lunch at my house every year. Last year, I misread the cooking instructions for the frozen turkey, so we had lunch at 6pm, by which time the vegetables were so overcooked that we had to bin them and resort to that famous festive combination: turkey with micro-chips and a side dish of Rudolph's tinned carrots. Still, at least the watered-down Bisto-tasting coffee will come in handy when we discover that, once again, we could grout tiles with my gravy.

Then – my toes are curling at the thought – the after-dinner powder keg. Some family get-togethers are blighted by drink. Some by deep-rooted feuds. Ours? Board games. My brothers and I have a genetic flaw – we can't be in the same room as Pictionary without erupting into a ferocious battle involving threats that would result in a trip to casualty to surgically remove a Christmas tree.

But peace will be restored when we re-bond over an ensemble rendition of 'Summer Nights' on the karaoke.

I'm Dreaming of a...

And at the end of the day, I'll crawl into bed, count my blessings and vow once again to add some special essentials to next year's Christmas wish-list: a chef, a house-keeper, a foolproof coffee maker, Kofi Annan and a NATO peace-keeping force.

Oh, and some kind of miracle cream for those bruised buttocks. ◆

Musical Toys and Domesticating Boys »»»

Growing Pains...

I want to make an official complaint to the MP for Motherhood. When I signed up for this whole parenting thing I was under the impression that I could look forward to at least sixteen years of unconditional love, footie games in the park, sneaking into Disney movies and using the kids as an excuse to go to Pizza Hut. And all it would cost me is a lifetime of mother's worry (breast or bottle, working versus stay-at-home, and will my cooking scar them for life?).

Apparently not. This week, a new study has revealed that childhood is effectively over by the age of eleven. Noooooooo. In future years, who's going to come with me to see *High School Musical 6* if my boys are too busy doing typical thirteen-year-old stuff like applying for their first mortgage and researching pensions?

Depressingly, though, I think the researchers have a point. In fact, in some cases childhood can end even earlier.

8 a.m. at the Low house: the air resounds with a panicked,

'Where's my hair gel?' Husband? Me? Er, no. Low the Elder, aged seven, he of the boyband barnet, the one who inherited his mother's shallow and superficial genes and prays every night to the Gods of Nike and Lacoste that I'll buckle and let him have designer trainers.

Although close in age at six and seven, my boys are at opposite ends of the maturity spectrum. My youngest still believes that you should regularly smother your mother with kisses, still sleeps with a menagerie of furry animals, and is saving up his pocket money so he can adopt Scooby Doo.

But the older one? Witness the scene: the noise of football studs marching down the hallway announces his arrival home from football training. He strolls into the kitchen and, with a casual, 'Hey Mum,' bypasses me on the way to the fridge. There he pulls out a fajita wrap, ham, and a tin of corn, plops them on a plate, pours a glass of fresh orange juice, closes the fridge door and announces, 'I'm just away to watch the game.' The game. That's the footie match on Setanta that he left a note for me to remember to Sky+.

He grabs the paper first every day to read the sports pages. He's happy to have a two-hour conversation about the merits of the transfer window system. When I'm clothes shopping, he taps his watch and tuts every few minutes. That's not a Primary 3 kid – it's a miniature middle-aged man.

How did this happen? In the age-old tradition of maternal guilt, I'm wondering if it's all my fault.

I've tried to avoid lavishing them with the perks of

adulthood; much to their disgust, they don't have TVs in their rooms, ditto DVD players, and I'm absolutely paranoid about the damage mobile phones may or may not do to the brain, so they won't be getting those until they're thirty. And at the first sign of fresh, dry air I still wrench them away from the computer games and prod them out the back door with a football.

On the other hand, however, I have encouraged the mature traits of independence and self-sufficiency, thinking that I was instilling valuable life skills. Since they could walk, they've been making their own beds, putting their clothes in the laundry basket and tidying their rooms. We haven't put them down a mine, but they do have to set the dinner table, clear up afterwards and pitch in with the housework. And my youngest, completely unprompted by us, has taken to making the packed lunches every night and running the Dyson round the kitchen. He'll make a lovely husband one day... as long as his new wife is prepared to accept the stuffed animals and adoption of Scooby Doo.

So, parents who've been through this, help me out here with the dilemmas of family life. How do I make sure that their childhood lasts as long as possible, while teaching them to be responsible and domesticated? How do I hold back the pressure to grow up too quickly? What, exactly, is the transfer window system? And if you can't answer with any of those issues, maybe you could offer some practical support – in a few years' time, fancy coming to see *High School Musical 6*? ◆

Making Sweet Music

I've come to a sad and shocking realisation – musical instruments are the work of evil.

What was I thinking? How could I ever have thought that giving two small boys (aged six and eight) instruments of volume could be a good idea? And why did no other parents (yes, that's a dig at any chums who are reading this) flag up that the introduction of a guitar and a keyboard into the family abode would be about as welcome as gastroenteritis and fleas?

It all started when Low the Elder asked Santa for an electric guitar for Christmas. I should have said no. I should have resisted. But I had a flashing image of how cool he'll be when he's eighteen, dressed in boots, hat and jeans, chewing a cocktail stick as he casually strolls into a party with his gee-tar over his shoulder. Memo to self: must seek help for country music addiction. Of course, in the cold light of day that's a ridiculous image – he'll be at least thirty by the time I allow him to walk anywhere with a stick in his mouth without screeching, 'Take that out right now in case you fall and swallow it!!!!'. I'm sure Johnny Cash's mother did the same.

Inspired by his sibling's success in the instrument-request department, my youngest son, aka 'Me Too' decided to get in touch with his inner Liberace and announced that he wanted a piano. Cue one letter to the fat bloke with the reindeers asking for his very own Steinway. With a backdrop of rising panic (and the thought of my bank manager rocking back and forward in the foetal position), I attempted to dissuade him with, 'Sorry, sweetheart, but a piano would be too big to fit on Santa's sleigh'. I thought I'd got away with it until he appeared the next morning in the closest thing he's got to a starry little lamé number (a Captain America costume) and said, 'Mum, if a piano is too big, how did Santa get the pool table here last year?'

Damn those superior superhero powers of logic.

This time, even husband diverted his attention from the holy wall box of Sky Sports for long enough to protest. He said it was a bad idea. He sat on his credit cards. He offered therapy. He threatened to cut off my Revel supplies. But did I listen?

No – because, inexplicably, my imagination kicked into overtime once more and my judgement was yet again clouded by notions of the future. My two boys both playing instruments? I was thinking Jonas Brothers (if you're over thirty, ask a teenager). Maybe even the next Osmonds (but without the extra brothers and the superior dentistry). Or Bros without that third guy.

What did we get? Oasis. Without the musical talent.

For the sake of marital longevity, I hereby offer an official public apology.

Come Christmas morning, Santa rustled up a keyboard and aforementioned electric guitar for the boys – the tinnitus for the parents came shortly after.

8 a.m. on Boxing Day, we were lying in bed being serenaded by what sounded like Liam and Noel Gallagher after a night on the batter, when husband nudged me. 'Hear that? It's the Hallelujah Chorus.'

'It sounds nothing like it.'

'I know that, but it's what all the neighbours will say when they're done.'

It's hell. With sound effects. They play in the morning. They play in the evening. The play so much that I keep telling myself that maybe they'll cross from noise pollution to a real tune some time in the next decade.

In the meantime, thankfully I've still got my oh-too-vivid imagination to see me through. I've dreamt up a whole new set of snapshots of the future… In every one of them, there's Liam, there's Noel and mum and dad are the ones in the earmuffs. ◆

The Bonnie Banks...

If last weekend was written in the poetic language of a travel brochure, it would go something like this: a glorious three-day adventure in the stunning setting of Loch Tay, staying in a log cabin and revelling in the freedom of the outdoors.

Oh, I can almost hear the gentle breeze blowing through the lucky white heather.

However, the reality can be summed up in slightly more succinct terms: Four women. Seven wee boys. Twenty-two wellies.

Yep, it was our biannual trip up north – just my three girlfriends, our offspring, and so much food that I wasn't sure if we were taking our children on a weekend break or providing catering support for a regimental invasion of Perthshire.

We'd spent months planning it, every conversation punctuated with an optimistic 'Just as long as it doesn't rain.' Yes, I know we live in Scotland. And, yes, I know that some people enjoy invigorating jolly japes in inclement weather.

I'm not one of them. I'm a comfort-seeking, 'shag-pile carpet and a mini-bar' kind of chick, who would rather spend ten hours in a lift with a bag of snakes than venture out in a meteorological situation that requires a cagoule.

Previously, the weather fairy has always come through for us, but this time we were ambushed before we even got there, when our two-vehicle convoy took an unscheduled detour via Meltdown Central. Heading back to the cars after a pit stop, laden with in-transit supplies, I attempted to load the usually laid-back six-year-old Low The Younger back into his seat. 'Don't want to sit there,' he huffed. Groan. It would have been easy to give in and reorganise everyone else to suit him, but I'm from the stand-your-ground school of motherhood – Lesson 1: weakness leads directly to mutiny and in no time they'll be gorging on E-numbers and stealing the car and the credit card for a trolley dash to Toys R Us.

'Honey, that's your seat and that's where you have to sit.'

He responded in a typically mature manner. 'Waaaaaaaaaaaaaaaaaaaaaaaa.'

Cue ten minutes of negotiation, strops and stamping of feet. Most of it mine.

'Could be worse, it could be raining,' I commented – just as the aforementioned fairy turned on the celestial taps and soaked us.

The only silver lining was that the downpour made the junior MP for Big Fat Huffington capitulate and climb in.

I clambered back behind the wheel, drenched but satisfied

that I'd established that the mothers were in charge and the weekend boundaries would be set by those of us with height, wrinkles and adult intelligence.

I was just about to move off when my phone rang. 'Everything okay?' asked my pal from her vantage point across the other side of the car park.

'Yep, sorry about that – ready to go now,' I declared, still triumphant in the victory for common sense.

'Then you might want to take your coffee off the roof of the car.'

My beamer illuminated the route all the way around Loch Lomond. In the rain.

We finally got there, made lunch, then played footie with the boys. In the rain. When it stopped, we dried them out and went off for a boat trip on the loch. In the rain. We got waterlogged while walking home. We cooked dinner, before playing tennis... in the rain. The next day, we spent two hours doing archery. In the rain. Then... you get the picture – it rained. For a whole weekend. And it was the kind of driving, pervasive rain that oozed into every pore. By the time we packed up I had the shivers, permanently soaked knickers and trench foot.

Would I do it again? Well, the boys had a fantastic time and the scenery was spectacular, but I'd need some cast iron guarantees before I left. Can someone let the weather fairy know that four mothers from Big Fat Huffington would like a word? ◆

The Music Man

HNC (Has No Clue) in Parenthood, Module 232: Just when you think you're getting the hang of this parenthood lark, the Gods of Reality Checks will throw a ruddy big spanner in the maternal works.

I knew it was all going too well.

I managed to survive those nine months of pregnancy, when I sweated like a seal in a sauna and grew to the size of the average portaloo.

I gave birth after a thirty-two-hour labour to a nine-pound son (and I'll remind him of both those facts on a monthly basis until the end of time).

Then I did it all over again a year later.

I survived the nappy years, then the potty years, then those endless afternoons fishing toddlers out of ball crawls and pondering whether I could cope with another episode of the *Teletubbies* without suffering a break in the psyche that leads to me shouting 'Eh-oh' at the postman (if you don't understand that last bit, ask any mother who had a preschooler between 1997 and 2001, but go armed with a large glass of vino and expect snot and hysteria).

I coped with 1,453 imaginary disaster situations as I sent them off for their first days at school.

I did the supportive mother/chauffeur thing at football, tennis and karate-type stuff and I didn't complain. Okay, I did. Loudly and regularly. But I still maintain that if women were in charge of football then it would be played in the summer instead of the winter, there'd be Danish pastries at half-time and all parks would have heated shelters at the side of the pitch, fully kitted out with co-ordinated soft furnishings, foot spas and tea-making facilities.

After much training and conditioning, I eventually educated them in the complicated rituals of the seat-up/seat-down lavatorial procedures – a skill that still hasn't been mastered by many fully mature members of their species.

And I've managed to get to this stage of my offspring's development without them succumbing to bad career choices, dysfunctional relationships or dubious personal habits. Which is just as well because they're only six and seven.

But just when I thought I had a ticket to sail on calm waters from here to Puberty Central, it's all – sob – gone horribly, unexpectedly wrong.

Low the Elder has done the unthinkable. He embarked on that chain of actions that strikes fear into the heart of every mother and father in the country. He – I can hardly bear to say it – saved up his pocket money and bought a recorder.

That whooshing noise you can hear is my will to live smothering itself in soundproof bubble wrap before diving into the nearest underground bunker.

A recorder! Apologies to anyone who has made devotion to that instrument of torture their life's work, but it's up there with nails scraping down a blackboard or an out-of-tune soprano singing opera. Backwards. With bulldog clips on her extremities.

Where, oh where, did I go wrong? Why couldn't he just have settled for a drum kit or bagpipes like any normal kid?

Parents, help me out here – there must be some kind of trauma-prevention system that will get us through this without loss of sanity, neighbours or eardrums. Please forward any advice to: S. Low, Parenthood Nightmare, c/o The Nearest Soundproof Bunker.

In the meantime, I'll plough on with my HNC (Has No Clue) in Parenthood. Hopefully, the next lesson will include practical steps to help preserve the bond between parent and child – Module 233: 'Musical Instruments and How To Lose Them'. ✦

2009

Christmas Letters and
Plans To Do Better ››››

Birth Plans

Birth Plans

National Health Warning: Menfolk, I hereby announce that the following article will contain references of a gynae-cological and reproductive nature. Placentas, episiotomies and birth canals may feature. Apologies if you were about to tuck into a sausage roll and have now lost your appetite.

Ladies – and the brave, hardy males who didn't just panic and flick straight to the next page – there are many things in life that I won't comment on or judge. And, yes, I'll ignore the snort of derision just emitted by the husband as he read that last sentence over my shoulder.

I've absolutely no idea how it feels for blokes to get a boot in the gahoolies, so I couldn't determine the appropriate reaction. Similarly, I'm thinking that a sack, back and crack wax is probably akin to a Brazilian, but I'm not sure so I won't compare the two.

Incidentally, I am now typing with my legs crossed.

So you'll understand, then, why I'm struggling (struggling

– meaning to experience the rising of hackles and irresistible urge to utter sentences containing the words 'bloody' and 'cheek') to accept the recent witterings from a male doctor who announced that women should not take any form of chemical pain relief during childbirth as the pain is a 'rite of passage' and a 'purposeful, useful thing' that prepares women for motherhood. Oh, and apparently having epidurals, gas or any other chemical pain relief also impairs a woman's ability to bond with the baby.

In the name of judgemental tosh, this ludicrous theory just made it onto the pregnancy popularity list somewhere between haemorrhoids and dodgy bladders.

Don't get me wrong, I'm a strong supporter of any woman who wants a natural birth. It's an inherently personal choice and every mother should be encouraged to make their decisions based on what's best for both mum and baby. When I showed up at Paisley Maternity Hospital ready to pop out Low juniors (by the way, whose sick idea was it to put a maternity hospital at the top of a coccyx-crushing big hill?), I had a solid, well-thought-out birth plan in mind.

Enter hospital.

Leave with my baby.

Everything in the middle was up for debate, depending on developments, personal feelings, the advice of the medical professionals and the level of toe-curling agony. In the end, I had epidurals with both babies. And, contrary to this latest nonsense, we all bonded just fine. I wish the esteemed gentleman had been there after the first thirty-two-hour labour to tell me how I was doing it all wrong. I'd have been all ears – right after I'd watched him shoot cricket balls out of a part of his nether-located anatomy normally reserved for another purpose.

As if we didn't have enough reasons to heap on the mother's guilt these days (childcare, E-numbers, organic diets, juggling family with career, etc.) without being castigated over our birthing techniques.

I'm also curious to know if this new theory that the lack of parental pain leads to bonding issues extends to the males of the species?

My other half felt absolutely no pain during the birth of our children – although that changed a few weeks later when I found out that when I sent him outside the delivery room to pace for a while, he actually nipped into the telly room for some tea and toast. His ears will have recovered from my reaction to that discovery at some point just before the end of time.

But will the fact that he didn't experience more than a wee twinge in his elbow as he lifted his mug mean his sons will avoid him in the pub in twenty years' time?

Or is the arrow of parental guilt and worry just aimed at the species with piles and stretch marks?

Sorry, but I'm not buying it. I think we should have new rules – formal legislation on who can give their opinions on all things pregnant.

Because I Said So

To paraphrase that famous old saying, thoust shouldn't judge a woman until they've walked a mile in her shoes… or had their legs in those stirrups. ◆

MP For Motherhood

David Cameron announced this week that anyone can apply to stand as an MP on behalf of the Conservative Party. No word yet on the criteria, but given the recent expenses debacle, I'm guessing candidates must know for sure what house they actually live in and display the ability to clean their own moat.

The current political shake-up has got me thinking that perhaps I should throw my chocolate Hobnobs into the ring. My family would, of course, be right behind me. I just told husband and his head is still on the kitchen table. The fact that I truly believe he's overcome with emotion and enthusiasm makes me deluded enough to match up to most of our current crop of bloated members.

So, yes, I'd like to be the MP for somewhere nice. Somewhere that I'll be proud to represent. Somewhere that embodies who I am and what I stand for. Shari Low – Member of Parliament for the county of Matalan and

Mothercare. I'll even have an emblem – I'm thinking of an ornate crest crafted from a photograph of two nipple shields and a breast pump.

Okay, so that last line just lost me the male vote.

But back to my motherhood manifesto. There would be rules. Serious rules. Number one – children must get up first time you wake them in the morning. It's the law. Note to Low junior: sticking one foot out of the bed and thumping the floor doesn't fool anyone.

Next on the list: packed lunches. Or, as they're known in this house, the work of evil. Healthy, balanced packed lunches will be delivered to every home first thing in the morning. This will, of course, have the spin-off advantage that the divorce rate will plummet. And husband, it's your turn tonight and, no, strawberry jam sandwiches don't count as one of the five a day.

The MPs' expenses fund will be reallocated to give all children a new pair of trainers every month because I'm going to have to remortgage the house to keep up with my boys' feet growth. The eight-year-old is a size five, the seven-year-old is a three. It gives me some comfort that, if they go for a comedy career with the circus, they'll be able to wear their own shoes to match the checked suit and the curly wig.

Ironing will be declared an illegal activity, punishable by two weeks of listening to Jeremy Clarkson talking about gear sticks and torque. The latter of which I'm led to believe has no relation to a seaside town on the south coast.

It will be prohibited for any stars to be photographed in full make-up and size-zero jeans until their babies reach an appropriate age. I'm thinking around seventeen will just about do it.

Every child will be trained in the musical instrument of their choice. As long as the junior Lows reject the recorder, the accordion or the bagpipes.

Heated shelters will be placed at the side of every football pitch in the land, because it's a miracle that I escaped six months of freezing, soaking Saturdays last winter without hypothermia and a foot infection.

All the money that is currently spent on useless, politically correct, bureaucratic pointlessness will be rechannelled to build a sports centre and a cinema in every town. And entry for families will be free.

Childcare will be regulated and 100 per cent subsidised by the government.

And most importantly, on the financial front, the going rate for the Tooth Fairy will be restricted to a national limit of 50p. A ban on moaning 'but Mu-u-u-um, my pal Steve got a fiver' will then be strictly enforced.

Forget the Tories, forget Labour, forget the Greens. Vote for me. I'm the MP for Matalan and Mothercare and I've got all the requirements for the job: passion, dedication, a desire to serve, two nipple shields and a breast pump. ◆

Eye Eye

Dear readers, I finally have a claim to fame. A truly unique achievement – one that sets me apart and may well put me in the history books.

Forget those common-as-muck Nobel Prizes. I haven't discovered a new planet. Or written a global bestseller. Or made it along the M8 without spending an hour in roadworks.

It's much, much more exclusive than that. I think I may be the only person in the country to end up in A&E after being injured by a theme park map.

I blame karma. Only a few months ago I was reading one of those daft hospital surveys that claimed something like 343 people ended up seeking treatment for a biscuit-related injury last year; 297 people were assaulted by a shoe box; and 111 people required hospitalisation due to a limbo-type activity. Oh, how I sniggered.

Little did I know that karmic justice would be swift and toe-curlingly painful.

Eye Eye

Last weekend, we took the junior Lows down to Alton Towers and the giddy excitement was palpable. The kids were quite chuffed to be going, too.

Within an hour of hitting the park, my pal Jan and I had wimped out of rearranging our internal organs by going on the Oblivion ride and were sitting on a wall having a coffee and a gab. While we discussed vital world issues (*X Factor*, *Strictly*, *America's Next Top Model*), seven-year-old Low the Younger consulted the map for our next death-defying activity.

'Look Mum,' he exclaimed, spinning towards us while clutching the park guide in his hands, 'There's a...'

I didn't hear the rest. I went down like I'd been hit by a catapult after experiencing the most excruciating eye pain. Somehow, in the most random event since Boaby from Auchtereejit was concussed by a Jaffa Cake, the corner of the map had sliced my cornea.

Honestly, I'd roll my eyes to heaven if both of them were working.

Husband came off the ride and looked at my crumpled form with an expression that sat somewhere between incredulity and suspicion. He'd just hurtled to earth at breakneck speed, yet I was the one requiring medical attention.

He was kind enough not to remind me that, on the drive down there, I'd nudged him and joked, 'Think we'll get through the weekend without ending up in hospital?'

Yes, we've got form for this kind of thing.

New York 2001: A&E, face injury caused by windstorm (mine).

Los Angeles 2004: A&E, Buzz Lightyear-sustained head wound while going to infinity and beyond (Low the Elder).

Florida 2005: A&E, suspected DVT (mine).

Cyprus 2006: A&E, suspected concussion caused by poolside slip (Low the Younger).

Ireland 2007: A&E, nerve damage to neck (mine).

And now, 2009: Alton Towers, mother clutching eye while pathetically screeching with pain.

Off to A&E we went, where my ailment was confirmed, treated and patched. Yep, patched. So, not only did I suffer the trauma of the injury, but I spent the rest of the weekend being subjected to small children asking me if I'd escaped from the pirate galleons and did I know Jack Sparrow.

Yet another episode of high-octane glamour and dignity.

I'm holding on to the small consolation that at least it makes me special. Unique. If I'm not personally named in one of those daft surveys next year, I'll be going to see the researcher in charge and I'll be giving him a piece of my mind.

Unless, of course, I get knocked out by a custard cream on the way there. ◆

Dear Santa

Altogether now: 'Jingle bells, jingle bells, jingle all the way…' Sorry, but I'm just doing my best to keep my Christmas spirit going. Usually, I love the festive season. I get all excited and start humming 'We Three Kings of Orient Are' somewhere around mid-November. However, this week a couple of challenges have scuppered my yuletide boat.

Rewind to last Sunday, and it was like a fairy-tale scene from a Christmas card in our house – if the Christmas card was one of those talking ones that opens with a chorus of 'who brought those bloody penguins out again!'

Yes, our three singing penguins had escaped from hibernation in the loft and were once again residing on the hall sideboard. They're loud, irritating, and the lowest form of entertainment. God, I've missed them. Unfortunately, husband, not so much. At one point, he got so irritated with them bursting into a rousing rendition of 'We Wish You a Merry Christmas' every time he walked past, he started muttering ultimatums about it being 'them or him'. We've taken to calling him Happy Feet in the hope that he'll mellow and accept that they're part of the family.

I eventually distracted him with the giddy joy of unleashing more seasonal tat. I asked him to put the outside decorations up, forgetting that every year it ends with him up a ladder, weeping with embarrassment while trying to balance a flashing reindeer, three neon elves and a set of icicle ropes on the roof.

However, at that moment I had bigger problems to deal with.

Just as I was about to talk him down and settle him in front of Sky Sports until the hysteria subsided, Low the Younger, aged seven, appeared clutching a sheet of paper. 'Here you go, Mum,' he announced. 'It's my letter to Santa.'

Aw, so sweet. My heart swelled with the festive excitement of it all. 'What have you asked for?' I cooed, ready for some kind of variation on the usual Lego/skateboard/bike combination.

'Lego,' he said. Tick. 'A skateboard,' he said. Tick. How well do I know my boy? I just waited for the final bike… Er, the bike. Come on, honey, add the bike.

'And a dog.'

Cue sound of large sleigh hitting crash barriers. A dog.

Blissfully unaware that I was now in a worse state than his penguin-and-tat-averse father, he ploughed on. 'And I've already got a name for it. I'm going to call him Murphy, after Gran.'

Dear Santa

It took me a moment to update my understanding of the situation. Apparently, the bike was out. Replaced by a dog. One that was called after my lovely granny who passed away two years ago. It was like a whole festive, family Greek tragedy. With tinsel and three singing Antarctic marine birds in the hall.

I realised that I had to handle the situation with tenderness and honesty.

'But honey, Santa isn't allowed to bring pets on Christmas Day. It's against the law.'

That would do it. Calm. Reasonable. Easy for him to absorb and accept. Until…

'No it's not,' came the reply. 'He brought my pal Ben a Dalmatian last year.'

Where are the Three Wise Men when you need them?

'You see, Mum, Santa can bring anything. You just write three things on your letter and, as long as you've been good, he brings them to you. You can ask for anything at all.'

Sigh.

Dear Santa,

On Christmas morning I'd like the following:

A marriage counsellor. A penguin protection order. And a really great excuse as to why there isn't a Dalmatian called Murphy sitting under my tree… ◆

2010

Costumes and
Dodgy Tunes ››››

The Horn

Consistency. Commitment. Dedication. Tenacity. They're all qualities that I try to drum into my boys. They're right up there with don't backchat your parents, be kind to your friends and this house doesn't come with a laundry fairy that transports your washing into that big white machine in the kitchen.

I want my offspring (aged eight and nine) to be grafters – the kind of kids that stick at things and don't give up when the going gets tough. For the purposes of this moral lesson we will overlook the fact that, since my oldest was born, I've been on approximately 1,675 diets and there isn't a piece of exercise equipment in existence that I haven't purchased, dumped in the corner of my bedroom and then reclassified as a clothes horse.

But back to the children. They have to see things through. Keep going through the hard times.

This week I realised that comes with an exception.

'Mum, can I give up playing my brass horn?'

If you live within a ten-mile radius of my postcode, you may have heard the exultant cheers.

Yes, the horn is dead. It's the musical equivalent of a lottery win for the ears.

Apologies to all you serious musicians out there who are accomplished in the ways of the horn, but one more night of Low junior marching up and down the hall playing an approximation of 'Twinkle Twinkle Little Star' would have tipped me over the edge.

There should be a law against it. Or a commandment. Thoust shalt not emit a noise that maketh thy mother's teeth grind.

Please don't judge me. I've always tried to be an encouraging, all-round supportive parent. I didn't complain when Low the Elder's participation in the wettest, muckiest football season in Scottish history cost me more Daz than Danny Baker could shift in a lifetime. I bit my tongue when a flirtation with martial arts ended in the destruction of my living room lamp, a sprained ankle and a request to change Low the Younger's name to Jackie Chan.

When Low the Elder took up the guitar and played 'Wonderwall' all night, every night, for a month, I dealt with the pain by convincing myself that we were a thick set of eyebrows and an arrogant swagger away from Oasis.

But then, like all good things, it spiralled out of control. The youngest decided he shared his brother's musical aspirations and got in on the act. I've no idea why. It certainly isn't a genetic predisposition. I can just about strum the best of the Beatles on the guitar, as long as it doesn't involve more than three chords and none of them require doing that 'bar' thingy with the index finger. And, while I adore my husband, I may have mentioned (at least once a month and usually when he's committed a marital crime like forgetting to Sky+ *Criminal Minds*), he's not a natural musician. If we used the rhythm method of contraception I'd be trading in the jalopy for a twelve-seater mini-van.

Anyway, the piano came next. Then the saxophone. And then horn. Or, as it's more commonly called, 'a migraine too far'.

Now that it's gone, I've learned my lesson and I'm drawing up new rules. No more musical instruments. No outdoor sports in winter. And our little Jackie Chan will be changing his name back pronto. From now on I'll be encouraging them to take up only quiet, indoor activities geared towards health and fitness.

They'll have a great time pedalling on that clothes horse. ◆

A Good Sport

The tension mounts as the athlete steps up to the starting line. Ready. Steady... A sheen of sweat forms on his face. Teeth clench. Muscles flex. Go! He takes off, thundering past the cheering crowd, evoking the spirit of those that have gone before him. Steve Ovett. Sebastian Coe. That bloke out of *Chariots of Fire*. As he crosses the finish line, the spectators roar.

Moments later he claims his prize – a Nobbly Bobbly ice lolly and a pound that is not to be spent on anything containing E-numbers.

It's that time of the year again – that melting pot of snot, sweat and tears that is school sports day. The junior Lows' big event is taking place this week and I'm already practising my parental mantra of 'it's not the winning, it's the taking part that counts'.

There's nothing worse than lining up to watch your child participate in a sporting endeavour and the peace being spoiled by a parent on the sideline who is acting like her wee darling is about to take part in an Olympic qualifier.

Okay, that's normally me. I'm sorry. I go with all the intention of maintaining a modicum of calm, magnanimous serenity and end up cheering (screaming like a banshee) and commiserating (roaring with disappointment) when the front half of the human wheelbarrow goes off in the wrong direction and crashes into the toilet tent.

It doesn't help that the Low brothers have very different attitudes to sport. My youngest has the competitive spirit of, say, mud. He couldn't care less if he doesn't achieve world domination in the egg and spoon race. He never reached a giddy pinnacle of success in his short football career because every time a teammate went down after a tackle, he ran over, applied first aid and attempted to put them in the recovery position until the paramedics arrived. He's a chilled-out homebody and his only chance of athletic stardom is if the International Athletics Federation introduces the new sport of sofa-surfing.

Then there's my other son. Usain Bolt. He has the competitive drive of a professional athlete, hates losing, and puts his heart and soul into every match and competition. He works out strategies. He trains. He pushes himself. And as long as he doesn't get signed for a premier football team or snapped up by the next big boy band (yes, we like to keep it real in this house) then he's aiming for Commonwealth glory in 2018.

But back at the sports day, all that junior endeavour and tension pales in the face of the most dreaded aspect of all: the parents' race. Or, as I like to call it, 'The annual exercise in disappointing the kids.'

There's always at least one Flo-Jo who shows up in full running gear and custom-made trainers and spends twenty minutes limbering up and mapping out the course. Just when the rest of us are trying to find someone to hold our coffees and cursing because we've forgotten to wear a sports bra again (well hello, back strain), Flo-Jo is up at the starting line being coached by the sports psychologist she brought along for support.

Someone really ought to have a word and tell her that it's not the winning, it's the taking part that counts. Although, I do reserve the right to change this viewpoint should a sport be introduced that plays to my strengths.

Ready, Steady...

Shari Low, Sofa-Surfing Champion 2010. ◆

Jolly Japes

Hear that noise? That's the unique sound of the final school bell and parents across the nation suppressing a panicked yelp.

Or is that just me?

Yep, school's out and my boys are about as calm as hyperactive chickens on a sugar rush.

Six weeks. Forty-two days. Deduct eight hours for sleeping and that leaves 672 hours to fill with productive activities. Sorry, I had to put my head between my knees until the urge to faint passed.

On the plus side, husband and I don't have to negotiate the annual trip to Divorce Threats Central as we attempt to pack and plan for a fortnight's jaunt to the sun. The combination of looming deadlines and a hugely expensive house flood has ruled out a summer holiday, so we're staying put.

But that doesn't mean that I don't have plans to fill those 672 hours. Oh, the things we're going to do. There are going to be so many jolly japes that me and the two junior Lows will feel like we've come straight from an Enid Blyton adventure... If Enid was a United Nations negotiator with special skills in tactical operations. You see, we already have a disparity on the logistics front.

I love my children more than words and, given the choice, I'd rather spend the day with them than absolutely anyone else – with the possible exception of a lingering fantasy involving George Clooney, free designer shoes and a donut shop. Don't ask.

But this year, at the ages of eight and nine, they've discovered that dreaded, terrifying new feature: their own opinion.

Where did my boys acquire those? And how do I send them back for a full refund?

I had it all worked out. In the next 672 hours I was going to bake cakes, play footie in the garden, have picnics in the park, go for long bike rides, paint, read books, and listen to them practising their piano and guitar. They finished school as normal boys, they'll restart in August as McFly.

Oh, and since I am late on a deadline, I also need to fit in writing a new novel and practising my very best martyr face so that I can appear suitably miffed when husband waltzes off to the office every day, leaving me to juggle working from home with full-time motherhood. No, he doesn't care, but I persevere on the off-chance that he'll notice and I can use it as bargaining power at a future date. I'm not proud.

Jolly Japes

But back to my plans. Unfortunately, the small Lows have different ideas.

Low the Elder wants to go go-carting (saw it in an advert), try rope climbing (saw it in an advert), visit Pontins (saw it in an advert) and journey to Atlantis in Dubai. Yep, he saw it in an advert. Note to self: make addition to summer task list – stop son watching adverts.

I approached my malleable, placid, easy-going Low the Younger in the hope of gaining an ally on the walking/reading/picnic front. 'What would you like to do this summer, honey?' I asked.

'Watch telly.'

'And…?'

'Nothing else. Just watch telly.'

I've a feeling there could be tears, tantrums and snot. And the boys might react badly, too. Still, I'm convinced that my parenting skills will win out and accomplish my mission to have an Enid Blyton experience. Once there were the Famous Five. Then came the Secret Seven. Welcome to the Summer Adventures of the Temperamental Three. ◆

Proud Mary Payback

Drum rolls and trumpets please. This week's top prize in the 'Surveys That Tell Us Things We Already Know' goes to… the academic bods who revealed that mums embarrass their kids. Seriously. Someone actually spent time and energy studying this. They could have saved themselves the bother and just phoned my boys.

My brood are under no illusion that their mother comes with a large dose of mortification.

Apparently, my pals and I doing our funky Tina Turner moves when Low the Elder performed 'Proud Mary' at a school concert put me firmly in the category of 'pure beamer'.

Actually, I was already there. And not just for being forty-three and still using the word 'funky'.

Shouting to ask him if he needed a hug after a dodgy tackle on the football pitch resulted in a beetroot face (his), rolling eyes (his) and weary mutterings of 'She's never coming here again.'

Sadly, the chronic shame wasn't mollified by my defence that Cristiano Ronaldo's mother probably did the same.

However, here comes payback.

Once upon a time, some deranged old crone with a penchant for monkey nuts came up with a way for children across the land to subject adults to excruciating psychological dread and anxiety.

Yes, brace yourselves for my annual rant about the hell that is Halloween – a festival with traditions that are up there on my peeves list somewhere between athlete's foot and anything involving Lycra.

The jokes are painful. The current favourite for this weekend is: 'What's yellow and dangerous? A canary with a catapult.'

Then there are the two hours in which I get fifty-seven Harry Potters at the door, who look decidedly unimpressed when I hand over an apple and fun-size Milky Way. They then proceed to loiter on the doorstep in the hope that I'll capitulate and supplement the nutritional treats with 50p.

Oh, and rumour has it that, in these days of oppressive Health and Safety, dooking for apples now requires the utilisation of a snorkel and a panic button.

But the bit that makes my teeth grind like Freddy Krueger's nails on a blackboard is the pressure of producing the costumes. It's one of those defining tests of motherhood. Result: epic fail.

According to reports this week, Tom and Katie Cruise

spent $6,000 on little Suri's fairy princess costume. Note to Tom – I'm available for adoption.

In our house, we take a slightly different approach.

'Muuu-uuuum, can I be a kangaroo this year?' asked Low the Younger.

A kangaroo. That fabled animal of witchery and wizardry.

Although, on the positive side, I sent up a prayer of thanks to the gods of fancy dress that it wasn't a giraffe, because that would require tracking down a seriously long toilet roll tube.

Back to the kangaroo. Cue a frantic search on eBay for brown fake fur. The postman was just heaving five metres of hairy fabric to the door when my wee darling announced that he'd changed his mind and he now wanted to be Dracula.

R.I.P. Skippy.

Unfortunately, the fabric was non-refundable so some swift manoeuvring and readjustments were required, but I think – with the help of some adaptations and a few economies with the truth – I've pulled it off.

So if you meet us on Sunday, be kind with the monkey nuts. Laugh at the joke about the canary. But please, please don't point out that vampires don't tend to wear brown fake-fur coats, or Dracula will be on the phone to those researchers informing them of the latest thing his mother has done to embarrass him. ◆

2011

Grooming Regimes and Holiday Schemes ››››

Hair Today

The atmosphere was tense. The pressure was mounting. Scissors in hand, the hairdresser looked decidedly apprehensive as the client sat down and announced, 'Can I have two centimetres off the back please, some shape around the sides, and the fringe has to be long enough for me to flick it, but not too long because I can't have it in my eyes when I'm playing football.'

The hairdresser? Me. The client? Ronaldo Low. My son. Aged ten. And his eight-year-old wee brother was next in line at Salon Low, with a list of coiffure demands that would make Lady Gaga seem low-maintenance.

I demand a steward's enquiry. I was under the impression that boys were largely reticent in the hygiene department until they got their first serious girlfriend, whereby they then divided all of their spare time between the shower and the Brut counter in Boots.

I may be showing my age there.

But the point is that I thought I had a few more years before they were nicking my deodorant and sneaking my hair gel into their sports bags.

Apparently not. Somewhere in the last couple of months, the junior Lows have been possessed by the Gods of Lynx and Justin Bieber and they're now more image-conscious than the imaginary love child of David Beckham and JLS.

It's actually making me wistful for those heady days when I had to bribe them with Top Trump cards to brush their teeth. I'm mourning those giddy times when I would leave a trail of Skips from their bedroom door to the bath in the hope that they'd voluntarily go within a few yards of soap. And I well up every time I think of those precious moments when I'd prise their socks off them to shouts of 'But Mum, they're not even dirty yet – I've only had them on for two days.'

How did this happen?

Low the Younger has always been strangely obsessed by dressing smartly. I blame *Bugsy Malone*. He watched it forty-three times over a weekend in 2007, and ever since then he refuses to leave the house unless he's wearing a suit and a pork pie hat.

He blew all the money he got for Christmas on a tuxedo jacket, so he's either going to be an orchestra conductor, a chauffeur or the best-dressed plumber in Glasgow.

However, I took comfort in the fact that, although he permanently looked like Boy at Burton, he still had punk-rock hair and fingernails that could have been picking potatoes.

Hair Today

Now? We had a ten-minute 'debate' in the beauty products aisle at Asda last week because I refused to cave in to a request for a coconut and vanilla toiletry set.

Meanwhile, his big brother is going to end up with lop-sided shoulders, because the repetitive flicking of his head to ensure perfect positioning of the aforementioned fringe is building up Schwarzenegger muscles on one side of his neck. He can speak like John Freida on the merits of mousse versus hair wax. And – sob – I caught him co-ordinating his socks and jumper last week.

I fear it's the first steps on that danger-fraught road to membership of a boy band and a starring role as Torso of the Week in *Heat*.

It's got to stop. We have to put an end to this grooming regime before the dog suffocates on the Elnett fumes in the kitchen. I'm off to have a long, relaxing soak and contemplate how to get them back across to the grime line… just as long as Ronaldo or Bugsy will lend me their coconut and vanilla bubble bath. ✦

This is Mum

I was going to write about something highbrow this week. I had every intention of debating a matter of international significance, like world peace, global warming or Paris Hilton's Chihuahua.

But my plans to be the next Kate Adie were scuppered by a devastating event closer to home. It's taken ten years, four months and fourteen days, but I've finally encountered that moment that every mother dreads. Oh, the heartbreak. The gut-wrenching pain. The call to the National Association of Motherhood to complain.

I caught the kids impersonating me behind my back.

'This is Mum,' I heard my ten-year-old whisper to his wee brother, before screeching, 'Where are my keys? Where's my phone? Where's my purse?'

At which point, the two of them buckled with giggles and I made a mental note to confiscate their pocket money until they reach middle age.

This is Mum

For the record, I don't screech. In times of stress, panic and lost items, I just calmly raise my voice to a pitch that could crack glass. It just so happens that it's a daily occurrence because I honestly think there's some supernatural force that moves my stuff around when I'm not looking.

I need Derek Acorah to pinpoint why everything I put down seems to get beamed up by a paranormal intervention.

There's a planet somewhere that's populated by thousands of odd socks, 546 pens, 34 umbrellas, several mobile phones, a few pairs of knickers, my black cardigan and the raffle tickets I bought from a guy who came to the door last month.

The only consolation is that usually things turn up eventually. This week, one of the great mysteries of the year was solved without bringing in paranormal help or the CID.

I once had a light-pull in the bathroom that had a gorgeous crystal bauble on the end. Please don't judge me – I never claimed to be anything other than eye-wateringly naff in my interior design skills.

Sometime over the Christmas holidays, the crystal bauble broke off and I carefully placed it in the black hole that is the kitchen drawer, to be repaired at a later date. When I went to retrieve it, it had vanished.

I searched. I tidied. I cleaned. I rearranged. I interrogated the children. I accused the husband. I may have uttered a mild screech. And the poor dog almost got done on charges of theft and sent to puppy borstal.

Eventually, I accepted that it was another one of those

things that was just inexplicably missing. I'd pushed the mystery to the back of my mind until mid-term break when the school sent home the children's work for the first few months of the year.

Piles of spelling exercises. Books full of sums. Colourful artwork.

And the star of the show? A junk robot – a two-foot-tall creature made of toilet roll tubes, cereal boxes and egg cartons. And, not that I'm biased, but our robot is special. It was undoubtedly a stand-out among its peers, a style maverick in a sea of recyclable goods, and it's all down to the fact that apparently Low the Elder was unable to resist giving it a unique finishing touch.

Our robot has a crystal belly button.

Mystery solved. And the combination of this discovery and the ignominy of hearing my boys impersonating me has caused a seismic shift in my attitudes. I'm going to chill out and stop fretting over lost goods. Instead, I'm just going to trust that, when Low the Younger brings home the farm he's building this term, it'll include my purse, my mobile phone, my keys, thousands of odd socks, 546 pens, 34 umbrellas, several mobile phones, a few pairs of knickers, my black cardigan and the raffle tickets I bought from a guy who came to the door last month. ◆

Costa Del Factor Fifty

Apologies to the Scottish Tourist Board, but I cracked. Last summer, we plumped for a 'staycation' and by the end of the school holidays my bank balance and my wellies were begging for mercy.

I'd rather spend a fortnight in a shark pool on a deflating lilo than repeat the experience, so I booked our blue complexions a week in the Costa Del Factor Fifty.

Sweet Gods of Ambre Solaire, the anticipation was thrilling, right up until I remembered that the holiday countdown is like prickly heat – you forget how irritating it is until you're heading back to the chemist and trying to work out the Spanish words for 'calamine lotion'.

Yep, despite enough planning to launch a military coup, I always end up setting off for the airport with hair like a burst suitcase, a wide-eyed deranged expression and a faint whiff of Toilet Duck.

As always, this year I vowed it would be much different. I would be organised, prepared, preened, plucked, and I was not setting foot on an aeroplane with a bikini line that could benefit from a shampoo and set.

At least, that was the plan. In the end, I finished work at 8 a.m., leaving me exactly twenty hours to shop, pack and mobilise my troops. Doddle.

Step one – hair. While I was making breakfast, I slapped on the monthly 'dye-out-of-a-box'.

I was on my way to a foxy shade of Kate Moss when a combination of a laugh and a flick somehow sent a yellowish blonde tress straight into my eye. After reacting in a cool, calm manner involving screeching panicked statements about being blinded for life, I dunked my face in water and headed for the optician. No permanent damage done, but my eye would sting for a day or so.

Off I set, looking like something out of *Pirates of the Caribbean*, for the next task of the day. 'Remind me to get you socks,' I told ten-year-old Low the Elder, at the start of a gallop around Matalan.

Two hours later, we made it home with T-shirts, shorts, jeans, swimmies, a natty cowboy hat … but no socks.

I suddenly realised that I'd forgotten to put on any fake tan, so I slapped some on and carried on with the next job.

I won't go into details here, but let's just say the new gizmo I'd bought for hair removal made my one good eye weep when I tried it on my oxters, so there was no way it was travelling below the Equator. I threw extra-large bikini bottoms on to my packing pile.

Next, I pulled out the mini-laptop that I take on holidays, only to discover the children had somehow managed to download a virus while playing something to do with fighter-pilot ducks.

I put the iron on the wrong setting and melted the blouse that I'd owned for approximately three hours.

Husband and I threw out our annual threats of divorce when he criticised my packing and refused to let me put anything in his case because he said 'it would crush stuff'.

I went in the huff – then sat on my case to get it shut and broke it.

We ended up in the loft at midnight, dragging out two floral cases we bought in Santa Ponsa in 1988.

Four hours later, the alarm went off.

Husband turned to look at me and screamed. My fake tan had somehow formed into a pattern that roughly resembles how the Earth looks from space. After a quick clean of the house, we set off for the airport – and yes, as predicted, we had hair like a burst suitcase, a wide-eyed deranged expression, a faint whiff of Toilet Duck. This was complimented by one good eye, a dodgy hair-dye job, a husband in the huff, suitcases from the Eighties, excess body hair, sockless weans, and a pigmentation issue that looked like the outline of South America on the left-hand side of my face.

But next year it'll be different. It will.

Anyone know the cost of a fortnight in a shark pool in July? ◆

Sunny Side Up

This week's newsflash from the research world comes from the land of canals and cafes with suspicious aromas. Slide into those clogs and slap on the sunscreen, because academics at a Dutch university have confirmed that we'd all feel a whole lot better if we went on holiday more often. They've obviously never vacationed with my brood.

In the summer we blew the overdraft abroad, so last week we decided to stay closer to home for the half term break. After the usual Olympic endeavour that ends with me winning a Gold medal in Heavyweight Suitcase Shutting, we set off in a northerly direction.

On the first night, we stopped at a picturesque hotel on the banks of Loch Tay. The Tourism Gods shone down on us as we relaxed outside on a terrace overlooking the water. Time to exhale. Relax. Revel in the serenity.

'Mu-u-u-u-m,' said Low the Younger (nine). I immediately switched to maternal high alert given that the number of vowels is in direct proportion to how much trouble he thinks he's in.

'I've locked the keys in the car.'

In a perplexing feat, he'd retrieved a can of Pedigree Chum from the boot, then pressed the automatic locking button to close it, leaving the keys inside with all our worldly possessions. Thankfully, we'd already removed Murphy the labradoodle.

After a failed attempt at breaking and entering by the AA, we slept in our clothes and woke up with dodgier breath than the dog.

By noon, a friend had brought the spare key from home and we travelled the last fourteen miles to our destination. Husband was unusually quiet until he turned to me with eyes glistening, clearly moved by the beauty of the scenery. My romance anticipation antennae began to bleep like a reversing bin lorry as I prepared myself for loving words.

'Have you got any painkillers? That filling I got last week is killing me,' he blurted.

I knew the situation was critical when he proceeded to delve into my handbag without the aid of a biohazard suit, popped a Paracetamol, then insisted we track down an emergency dentist.

On day three, the holiday spirit, the sunshine, and the antibiotics for husband's abscess finally kicked in. Energised and happy, the junior Lows spent endless hours enjoying water sports on the Loch.

Later that night, I was just drifting off in a wee bubble of bliss when I was woken by ten-year-old Low the Elder. 'Mu-u-u-u-m.' Cue return of maternal alert as I immediately realised that his vowels were in proportion to how bad he was feeling.

'Are you okay, sweetheart?'

There was a two-word reply: Projectile. Vomit.

I spent the next thirty-six hours impersonating Florence Nightingale. If Flo was a slightly cranky Scottish woman who forced the brave warriors in the Crimea to watch back-to-back instalments of *Star Wars*, while she broke off from a Jackie Collins bonkbuster to rub their hair and blurt, 'Are you feeling any better yet?' on a ten-minute loop.

On day five, all pain and illness abated, legions of pals arrived to meet us. By nightfall, there was a veritable clan. That's when it happened. 'I've booked a treat for us,' husband announced.

Cue yet another traumatic event. White-water rafting, during which – sob – they made me pour my considerable curves into a wetsuit.

I won't comment any further, other than to say that we now have physical evidence of the stretch capacity of rubber, and there's a legendary creature in a loch slightly further north who may have a lookalike pal to keep her company.

On day seven, as we drove home in the pouring rain, I reflected that friends, family and sunshine had made our trip unforgettable. But I've decided to ignore the research that says we should vacation more often. For the sake of our health, my ego, our bank balance and the poor souls who were forced to witness an enraged, chunky tourist in a wetsuit rising from the deep, I'll be parking my clogs at home for the foreseeable future. ◆

Monaco

Ten years, ten months and two days. No, that's not how long I've been trying to shift the baby weight. Actually it is, but that's not the point. This month, after more than a decade, I finally reached another one of life's milestones – the husband and I went off for a forty-eight-hour mini-break without the kids.

So much for the recent vow to avoid trips for the foreseeable future, but in my defence dear bank manager, it was an impulse buy on a discount website. Also – yes, this is the mother's guilt trying to justify my actions again – the trip was primarily for work purposes. The final scenes of my current novel-in-progress are set in Monaco, and first-hand knowledge is essential when giving a story a dramatic setting. At least, that's what I tell myself when I dream of setting a book in Ryan Gosling's shower.

I was, therefore, fully justified in heading off sans-offspring. Nevertheless, a wave of anxiety almost had me tearing back through the departure lounge shouting, 'but I can't remember if I put a banana in my boy's packed lunch!'

Not that this was a *Home Alone* situation featuring Joe Pesci attempting to burgle a house in a Glasgow suburb while my sons foiled his plan with two tins of spaghetti hoops and a colander. As a neurotic worrier, every detail of their care was pre-planned with military precision. They went to live with my lovely pals, armed with a 128-point checklist, including a full medical history, a note of their blood type, a map to the nearest nuclear bunker and the phone numbers for emergency services, Interpol and NASA.

There were tears. Wobbly lips. Distraught expressions. But they were all in my pessimistic imagination. The junior Lows skipped away, thrilled that they were having a double sleepover.

I've been to Monaco twice before. Eleven years ago, husband and I got the bus there from our ramshackle hotel in a nearby town and sat in the Café de Paris, dreaming of riches. I had just landed my first book deal and naïvely assumed I'd have Jackie Collins's life before the week was out.

And I did! If Jackie Collins lived in Glasgow and had an overdraft the size of Mull.

Last time I visited the millionaire's playground was on an organised day trip. I arrived with a busload of very nice American tourists and realised that my blue and white striped T-shirt was a chronic fashion blunder. I was going for nautical. Instead, I looked like a deck chair in distress.

Monaco

The indignity was compounded when the heavens opened and we all got drenched, and then walking through the uber-glamorous Casino Square I slipped, went down like the Titanic and had to rely on ageing gentlemen with names like Buddy and Al to form a four-man hoist to get me up.

But this time was going to be different. Husband and I had packed our best togs. I'd painted my nails. The blue and white T-shirt had been binned. I'd even shaved my legs. We were child-free, and determined to be so suave and sophisticated that no-one would guess we didn't belong in such glamorous surroundings.

Oh yes, we were cosmopolitan travellers of the world. Until we got there, ordered two drinks and got a bill for £32. Husband just about fainted, but I didn't notice because I was too busy trying to Skype the kids. Cue a weekend of jaw-dropping bills, credit card stress and chronic worry that a meteor would hit the west of Scotland, wiping out the family I'd left behind.

We're obviously just not cut out for jet-setting à deux.

So I've decided to leave my next research trip for another ten years, ten months and two days. It'll take that long to get over the guilt, save up for a round of drinks and track down the location of Ryan Gosling's shower. ◆

We Wish You a Sherry Christmas

It started off as one of those beautiful family moments that makes you feel all warm and bubbly.

'Mum, I've to give a speech in class about our family traditions,' announced nine-year-old Low the Younger.

Aw, so cute. I immediately thought of all those quaint little things we do every year. Putting the tree up while singing along with *Now That's What I Call Christmas 5,675*. Hanging up the Christmas stockings. Donning my Santa suit and revelling in the fact that it's the only day of the year that I don't have to hold in my stomach. Opening the pressies one by one in strict rotation, dragging the whole process out for so long Santa is already halfway through a post-festive fortnight in Benidorm by the time we've finished.

'That's lovely sweetheart. What are you going to talk about?'

I said a silent prayer that he didn't mention our more controversial traditions – the Pictionary draw to the death and the standard ructions when my over-competitive siblings get out the Trivial Pursuit, then deny they've been memorising the answers since October.

His wee face lit up as he listed his subjects. 'Our tree...' Tick. 'Our presents...' Tick. 'My stocking...' Tick. '...and how you destroy the dinner every year.'

The latter was accompanied by hoots of hilarity from my wee elf and his eleven-year-old brother.

Woe. Holy Wolfgang Puck, it's a sad day when the offspring are using my culinary inadequacies as fodder for classroom hilarity.

I'm a forty-four-year-old, capable woman. I manage to hold down a job, raise a family, keep abreast of global affairs and follow the intellectual intricacies of *CSI Miami*.

Yet every year I go to battle with a turkey dinner and every year I slink away, defeated, clutching a handful of chipolatas and a hastily heated-up slice of emergency deep-pan pizza.

There's more chance of me rigging up another Hadron Collider in my shed than there is of mastering the complexities of the traditional festive feast.

There was the year that one too many Buck's Fizz (that's the drink, not the burdz that whip off their skirts while singing a Eurovision hit from the Eighties) resulted in temporary amnesia and I forgot to switch on the oven. Cue a phone call to summon chicken kormas for twelve.

The following year I managed to burn the whole thing to a crisp.

Then there was the time that the trimmings were perfection. Just a shame they were ready an hour and a half before the turkey.

None of which was as embarrassing as the time that the homemade soup somehow went off, and tasted like stewed reindeer dung.

Or the legendary year that my dearly beloved broke two veneers on my chipolatas.

And yet, still they come. At noon on the 25th, I'll be setting fourteen places at the table. I've realised that it's my family's equivalent of extreme sport – unpredictable, adrenalin-fuelled and potentially hazardous to health.

This year, I'm determined to succeed. I've written a list. I've checked it twice. I've banned the Bucks Fizz, and organised everything with the logistical detail of Santa's delivery schedule.

However, if it all goes wrong yet again, I'm going to remain positive and focus on the educational aspects of the day. We might celebrate the occasion with a non-traditional mighty meat feast, but at least Low the Younger will have another story to tell his classmates. ◆

2012

Beyoncé, Kate Middleton and Judy Murray Walk Into a Playgroup... ››››

Broody

Ladies, I have a crisis on my hands.

This is worse than the time I face-planked in the playground and my kids pretended they didn't know me.

It's worse than the time that Low the Younger's homemade Frosty the Snowman costume went wrong and the audience were perplexed as to why there was a singing penguin at the school Christmas show. Happy Feet Low has never recovered from the embarrassment.

It's even worse than the day that Elvis, our goldfish, went to the big bowl in the sky and I topped the insensitivity scale by serving up fish fingers for tea the next night.

The current situation is much more serious. Yep, it's the B-word. I'm… broody. That thumping noise is my biological clock chundering like a box of Pampers trapped in a tumble dryer.

This revelation has terrified the husband. In fact, I'm fairly sure that the only thing preventing him from leaving me is that there's only a couple of weeks until Superbowl Sunday, so even if Kelly Brook showed up in her knick knacks carrying a case of Budweiser, he wouldn't be tempted away from his fifty-inch plasma telly.

Instead, he's giving me wary glances and keeping a minimum of three feet away from me at all times in case I miraculously manage to get impregnated while passing him a cup of tea and a Tunnock's Teacake.

The cause of this hormonal surge is glaringly obvious. Welcome to the world, my three-week-old niece, Amelia. Naturally, I'm not biased in the least – she really is the most beautiful, funny, smart baby that the stork ever delivered. And I'm sure she's got my thumbs.

I expected to do that whole 'lovely, but nice to give them back' thing. But, no, I'm visiting so often that the little angel's first words are going to be 'restraining order for the overbearing auntie, please'. Her parents are increasingly scared to open their curtains in case my face is pressed up against the window.

I can't help think that Mother Nature is having a laugh. I'm forty-four. Knackered. There are bits of me that don't work any more. It's not even as if my pregnancy experiences were a thrill. I didn't bloom and glow. No, I lumbered and sweated. By the time my sons were born, I was so huge that Health and Safety insisted I made a beeping noise when I backed out of a room.

And after extreme pregnancy weight fluctuations and two

prolonged stints of breastfeeding, my breasts have gone from a 36C to a 42 Extra Long.

My boys are eleven and nine now, so I'm at the blissful stage where they are self-sufficient and independent but haven't hit the teenage years when they'll start crossing the road when they see me coming.

This should be an era of contentment, yet every time I see that gorgeous little face I catch myself pondering the plus sides of adding to the Low brood. That intoxicating baby smell (the baby powder one – not the one that requires investigation while wearing a gas mask). The joy that comes with every smile. And the social life. I could hang out with Beyoncé and we could go to baby classes together. She'd have wee Blue Ivy and I'd take my Scottish equivalent, wee Tartan Thistle.

I'm just praying that the logical side of my brain will wrestle control back from my hormones sometime soon.

Perhaps a few days of babysitting will put things into perspective and reduce the high-grade broodiness. Or maybe I should divert my maternal instincts elsewhere. I think it might be time to buy a new goldfish. I just need to find one that's got my thumbs. ◆

Suck It Up

Well, slap my thigh with a soggy Marigold.

According to a new survey, women spend three hours a week redoing housework that blokes haven't done properly. What a disgrace. This dirty dig at the domestic skills of the British male is patronising and downright insulting.

And I intend to spring to the defence of our menfolk, just as soon as I've finished re-mopping the kitchen floor that Low the Elder allegedly cleaned this morning.

Given the state of it, he clearly used an old mop. Or the dog.

I suspect he's hustling me. It's that old 'if I do it badly she won't ask me again' ruse, but I'm not falling for it. You see, my boys are already fully trained in household management. Tiger Mothers, read this and weep. Your offspring might be able to speak seven languages and play Vivaldi's *Four Seasons* on the harpsichord, but my boys know one end of the Toilet Duck from the other.

Suck It Up

It's obviously genetic. Anthropologists this week revealed that our ancestors – called hominins – started to walk on two legs instead of four because they had to carry food. I disagree. I reckon Mama Hominin Low served up dinner then insisted that Kiddy Hominins get off their prehistoric bahookies and carry their own plates to the dishwasher.

Educating my brood to HNC level in Household Sanitation was a conscious decision. Ever aware that I will one day be the needy, overbearing mother-in-law from hell, it was a token gesture to ingratiate myself with my future daughter-in-laws. I can only hope the fact that their husbands load the dishwasher will go some way to increasing their tolerance levels when I show up for my tea three times a week and invite myself on their annual holiday.

There were other motives, too. I'm a raging hypochondriac who lives in constant fear that exposure to a sink of dirty dishes will result in dengue fever and possible death.

Then there were the terrifyingly vivid nightmares in which my boys hit their teens and retreated into their bedrooms, where they lived in a cesspit of cola cans and Pot Noodle tubs until I stormed the room in a bio-suit shouting, 'Stand back, I'm coming in and I'm armed with Febreze!'

But, most importantly, I hate housework with a passion. It's up there with diets and anything to do with Gwyneth Paltrow.

I'm in absolute agreement with American writer, Erma Bombeck, who once said, 'My second favourite household chore is ironing. My first being hitting my head on the top bunk bed until I faint.'

The only redeeming feature of domestic servitude is that it burns up calories. But, then, so does pole vaulting and I've so far managed to avoid using the whirlie gig to catapult myself over the garden wall.

Taking all of the above into account, sharing the household tasks seemed like a sound plan, and occasional work-dodging ruses aside, my offspring have accepted that they have to do their bit with the duster. I'm sure that somewhere up there in the squeaky clean prehistoric clouds, Mama Hominin Low is looking down at us and beaming with pride.

So purveyors of inane surveys, lay off my menfolk. Their housekeeping skills may not be perfect but I can sleep easy at night knowing that no woman will ever have to clean up after them. I'm convinced that their domestic education and their Marigolds will see them through the important and demanding times ahead of them – their student days, married life, and the three days a week that their overbearing mother comes for tea. ◆

Good Morning?

Reasons I'll never pass my HMC (Higher Maternal Competence) in Parenthood, number 1,264 – mornings.

When the kids were small they were a nightmare, but I thought they'd get easier as the years went by. Er, nope.

I've decided I have no alternative but to take legal action against those cereal companies with adverts depicting a happy little perfect brood sitting around the breakfast table, eagerly discussion what jolly japes they'll get up to that day.

In our house, there's more the atmosphere of a COBRA summit ten minutes after Martians have landed and announced plans to take over the world – somewhere between panic and sullen resignation.

Is it just me? Is this the only household in the world where mornings are about as much fun as a sudden bout of salmonella? We're rushed. Disorganised. Grumpy. And – oh the shame – more than once we've been so late that jammy toast has been consumed in the car.

Not one member of my family is a morning person. In my formative years, I was a nightclub manager and I blame those long hours of hardcore nocturnal endurance for the fact that my body still thinks it should stay up until 3 a.m. while planning my future life with Simon Le Bon. No-one has informed my internal clock that I'm now a mother with sole responsibility for getting two boys to consume copious amounts of Shreddies then get them out the door in a clean and organised state.

Sadly, our sons have inherited my genetic failings. At eleven, Low the Elder only talks in grunts before 8.30 a.m., and his normally chirpy wee brother has the demeanour of Gordon Ramsay in a burger van. Even the labradoodle views the alarm clock as a vessel of evil.

It almost makes me nostalgic for those younger days, when mornings involved me chasing them around seven circuits of the house with a face sponge and soap, and loud yells demanding that they stop playing football in the house or I'd confiscate the goalposts: a table lamp and the ironing board.

This week was gearing up to be even tougher than normal, being the first week back after Easter. After a fortnight of late nights and long lie-ins, we were about as motivated as mud, so I called a family meeting on the last day of the break.

'Right boys,' I announced. 'Tomorrow morning we're going to get up early and leave the house calm and happy.' They both looked at me with expressions of suspicion.

Good Morning?

I've never before used 'mornings' and 'happy' in the same sentence.

How hard could it be? I'm the woman who is obsessively organised at all other times. I can arrange a party for 300 at an hour's notice. I can entertain a dozen bored kids for hours. I can navigate IKEA without getting lost. I just had to find a way to manage cohesive thinking before 9 a.m.

I was determined that triumph would be mine – until I was foiled by yet another bastion of malice: the snooze button. Why were they invented?

After at least six semi-conscious taps of the little silver nub, I woke up half an hour late, and despite my vow to be a serene earth mother, I ended up getting louder and louder until the boys attempted to mute me with the remote control for the telly.

The end result?

Jammy toast in the car.

So fellow parents, I give up. I'm convinced it can't be done. I've decided that we're the normal ones and all those fictional family breakfast adverts are nothing more than cereal company propaganda.

I fully intend to contact my lawyer and arrange a meeting with a view to suing under the trade descriptions act.

Just as long as he can see me in the afternoon. ◆

Tennis Elbow

There are very few men I'll lose sleep for. My sons, obviously. My husband (although in his case there usually has to be a pay off involving dinner or the promise to put the wheelie bin out). Liam Neeson would, of course, make the list.

And now, step forward Andy Murray. Actually Andy, make it more of a shuffle than a step because your bones must be aching after winning the US Open.

Brad Pitt could have been waiting with a rose between his teeth and I still wouldn't have switched the tennis off the other night.

Wasn't Murray brilliant? Okay, so he doesn't ever make it easy for himself or for those of us willing him on from the high-pressure environment of the sofa. Or, in Alex Ferguson's case, sitting in the stadium like the sporting world equivalent of an enforcer, ready to dish out the hairdryer treatment if Murray looked like failing.

My nerves were shredded. I shouted at the telly. On several

occasions I required the calming properties of a hot beverage and a Kit Kat Chunky. And when he lifted that cup, I emitted a screech so piercing the neighbours immediately called Crimestoppers. But it was worth every excruciating moment.

However, there was one other person at the match who should have been doing a lap of honour with a trophy held aloft.

I hereby dedicate a golden MASK award (Mother of A Sporty Kid) to the irrepressible Judy Murray.

Judy has been much criticised over the years, accused of being a pushy parent and maligned for her dogmatic dedication to her son's career. Isn't that missing the point?

Year after year she ferried him to matches, washed his kit, cheered him on and stood in the pouring rain watching wee Andy batter a ball across a net.

And now that she gets to jet to New York and hob nob with Sean Connery, she gives hope to the rest of us, standing in the rain on touchlines all over the nation, slowly developing hypothermic tootsies while mentally working out how many times we'll have to soak the offspring's socks to get the grass marks out.

My eleven-year-old spends every evening and weekend partaking in some combination of tennis, football, basketball and the 100-metre escape from an embarrassing mother. The last one isn't yet an official sport but he's been practising ever since he was six and I stood in a goalmouth holding a brolly over him so he didn't get a chill.

The image of Judy punching the air this week will keep us parents of sporty weans going through another winter of Saturday morning fixtures, sub-zero temperatures, thermal knickers and chattering teeth. We can picture her joy when we're dizzy with euphoria that a week of galloping up and down the garden has paid off and our wee angels have finally managed to bend it like Beckham.

We can channel her relief when we're using two ten-foot barge poles to transfer rancid sports kits from a bag to the washing machine.

Behind every sporty kid there's a mum or dad, clutching a water bottle and forking out for petrol money, so Andy's parents deserve to revel in every second of his triumph.

I couldn't care less what career Low the Elder chooses, as long as he's happy. But if he does become a professional sportsman, I plan to be just like Judy, in that stand, cheering him on, making sure he's got everything he needs to play his very best.

Anyone know how I can book Mr Ferguson and his hairdryer? ◆

Royal Bumps and Blue Bits

Doesn't it make you swell with pride when there's a royal story that doesn't involve pixelated pictures of Harry's blue bits?

This week, the world's media bypassed the global financial meltdown, war, famine and those two married news presenters who are up to no good, to inform us that Kate had a new hairstyle.

And then – cue a baby names sweepstake in the office – came the announcement that our future king and queen are going to become Maw and Paw Windsor.

It's lovely news for the newlyweds, although there's a strong possibility that Christmas dinner with the relatives will be interrupted by Airmiles Andy throwing his rattle out of the pram because he's been shoved further down the queue for the big chair and the crown.

As with any pregnancy revelation, my thoughts flew to

that blissful day, twelve years, nine months and twenty-two days ago, when I discovered that my feelings of nausea were not caused by a post-Saturday night reaction to chicken balti.

After years of fertility treatments and disappointments, I was thrilled when the line appeared on the stick. Ecstatic. But there's no denying that, by the time Low junior entered the world, the husband had discovered many new things about his wife.

So your Royal Highnesses, just in case you are reading this, I would like to pass on some pearls of wisdom from a commoner who's been there, done that and scooped the baby rice off my best silk shirt.

The Lows' Top Ten Pregnancy Lessons:

1. My dearly beloved learned that a woman can be happy, overwhelmed, worried, loving, furious and hungry at the same time. The chance of accurately guessing which of these is the overriding emotion at any given moment is up there with Pippa's new book winning the Nobel Prize for Literature.
2. When faced with a hormonal female with the emotional stability of a seesaw on the San Andreas fault, make her tea, tell her she's gorgeous and then retreat to a nuclear bunker.
3. A balanced diet is essential. This may take the form of equal-sized bowls of pickled onions and custard. Consumed at 4 a.m.

4. A previously happy-go-lucky woman can become wracked with worry and uncertainty. But whatever the question is, no, husband, ginger bloody biscuits are not the answer.

5. While in the swirls of a hormone surge, she may develop unusual opinions on the perfect moniker for your imminent arrival. Agree to go with little Pickles Walthamstow McNugget until the next swirl adjusts her views.

6. It's common for a woman to glow and radiate contentment as she prepares for the miracle of birth. Unfortunately, I was the exception, who bypassed glowing in favour of sweating, swelling and waddling like an Emperor Penguin with polar piles.

7. In some cases, couples will re-categorize their profanities. Forget the F-word and the C-word. The major curses become the S-word (stirrups) and the E-word (episiotomy).

8. It's wise to prepare for the fact that a bump may come and go, but changes to the bosoms can be permanent. I believe the term 'landslide' is applicable.

9. Pregnancy does not automatically transform a female into Mother Earth.

I became her evil twin sister: Mother Volatile.
And, finally, all of the above can be helped by avoiding

stress, utilising the resources available to you, and accepting help.

So on behalf of Maw, Paw and the future babe, Pickles Walthamstow McNugget Windsor, I'd be happy to let Airmiles Andy know he's off the guest list for Christmas dinner. ◆

2013

Auntie's Tanks and Mothering Thanks ››››

Auntie

'An army of aunties.' I love the mental image that conjures up – a line of fearless women in khaki, ready to storm Matalan's car park if they can just work out how to parallel-park their tanks.

This probably isn't what author and child psychologist, Steve Biddulph, meant when he extolled the need for an aunt army to help guide today's girls through the complex trenches of the teenage years.

According to Biddulph, teens are under more pressure than ever before, and to give them an adequate support system, a duty of care should be extended to include other female relatives who can be confidantes and mentors.

Could someone let the head of the aunt army know that I'm volunteering for the task?

I have several gorgeous nieces and two teenage cousins that I adore.

At Christmas, my cousins stayed with me and, as always,

we spent our days in the kitchen drinking tea as I grilled them on every aspect of their lives. If the CIA would like to get in touch, my interrogation skills are available for the nominal fee of a bag of Tetley teabags and several packets of Hob Nobs.

In many ways, my young relatives' experiences mirror what I can remember of my youth. The flashbacks get hazier with every passing decade but there were definitely big dreams, self-esteem dips, boys, giggling friends and, in my case, a fantasy relationship with Jon Bon Jovi that stopped just short of a restraining order.

But back to my girls. Over the coming years, I plan to be there for them, always ready to listen without passing comment, delivering lectures or boring them with diatribes of advice. However, I'm aware that this kind of restraint would involve the application of gaffer tape to my gob, so I've already started preparing a checklist of the wisdom that I'd like to share as they embrace adulthood.

- Don't waste your time with diets. You're beautiful as you are. And besides, I've tried 4,396 of them and none worked.
- You're allowed to date one unsuitable bad boy, but after that, always go for the good guy.
- Pick great friends who will laugh with you, cry with you, and hunt down that bad boy if he breaks your heart.
- Don't photograph everything you do and put it on

Facebook, Twitter or Instagram. And don't pout in pics – it gives off a toxic air of Eau de Attention Seeker.

- Be careful with fashion, as things come back to haunt you. We call this concept The Curse of the Mullet.
- Make mistakes. Loads of them. At your age, we'll forgive you.
- Always stay true to yourself, and when it's time to choose a career, find something you love to do and make it your job. Please note this does not apply to touring the country attending One Direction concerts.
- There's a Brazilian wax and there's a Brazilian blow-dry. These are two very different things.
- Never do the running. If a relationship is meant to be, it will happen. Evidence of this theory can be found by turning to history and consulting the ancient classics. Start with *An Officer and a Gentleman* featuring Sir Richard of the Gere.
- And, finally, learn to tolerate the eccentricities of your older relatives. I'll be intrusive. I'll scan your social network sites. I'll turn up at parties. You'll leave a nightclub and find me there, waiting to give you a lift home. It's because I love you, not because I'm trying to ruin your life.

Oh, and when you're all grown up and I come to visit, persuade me to take a taxi. There's no telling what carnage I'll cause if I bring the tank. ◆

Second Time Around

This week's research from the University of the Blatantly Obvious?

A new survey out this week claims that one-fifth of mothers spend less money on their second child than they do on their first.

Shocker!

I can categorically say that I treated my two children completely the same. Not a penny of difference. And on the non-financial side, there was absolutely no disparity between the time I devoted to them. Definitely not. No way. Cross my heart and swear to the Patron Saint of Huggies.

Okay, there was, but please don't tell Low the Younger because I reckon he's the one that's most likely to pick me up from the Home for Decrepit Bonkbuster Authors and ferry me between the bingo and the line dancing, before whisking me to the garden centre for a cappuccino and a fruit scone.

I have always loved my boys absolutely equally, but there

was a huge difference between my preparations for number one and two.

Prior to the arrival of Low the Firstborn, I spent months planning every little detail. I painstakingly decorated his room down to the very last fluffy white cloud that I painted on the pale blue walls. Admittedly, I was never brilliant at art, so his cloudy skyscape actually looked like sheep in flight, but the effort was there.

I bought every baby gadget and gizmo ever invented, including a steriliser that was so high-tech it could eradicate germs and then act as a space probe to Mars.

I pored over every baby book ever written, and when he came along I kept a diary and charted every step and word of progress. When he cried, I lifted him. At night, I rocked him to sleep. And should he ever become famous, photo shoots will be second nature, as he couldn't toddle across the garden without me snapping pictures from behind a bush like a rogue paparazzo.

I wasn't so much a Helicopter Mother as a Mosquito Mum – buzzing around him incessantly and impossible to shift.

My second came along sixteen months later, and I'd love to say that I was the same bundle of maternal energy. Cue reality check.

I went from focused, organised mother of one, to a knackered mother of a baby, and an over-energised toddler who could do a hundred-metre dash in a time that rivalled Usain Bolt.

Low the Younger only got photographed on birthdays and special occasions. I was so tired and fuddled I'm fairly sure the camera was in the freezer next to the hairdryer and the house keys.

I've no idea what I did with his first tooth. I'm fuzzy as to what age he was when he walked and talked.

He wore clothes that his brother had grown out of. Played with toys his brother had left behind.

Oh the shame and large dollop of mother's guilt – the same one that kicks in every time a new study informs me of another thing I did wrong.

And yet… Son number two is the most laid-back, wonderful, contented wee soul ever. He doesn't stress, he's utterly non-materialistic, thoughtful and low-maintenance.

I may have spent less money on him when he was a child, but I was also more relaxed and confident and I think that rubbed off. Most importantly, love was always doled out to both of them in equal measure.

So, Son the Younger, I hope you forgive me and accept my apologies that there wasn't as much one-on-one time.

I promise that over the course of our lives I absolutely intend to make up for it.

Between the bingo, the line dancing and the garden centre, I'll be all yours. ◆

Party Popper

Hear that trundling noise? That's a bandwagon shooting past before I had a chance to jump on it.

Given that I'm prone to enthusiastically embracing superfluous trends, I'm gutted that there's now a veritable feast of modern celebrations and traditions that I missed, due to being born too close to the era when dinosaurs ruled the earth.

There's the primary school prom party. I'm not saying that I agree with spending £500 on a kiddie Gucci party frock and transporting your offspring to a school dance by helicopter, but it beats my last day of school which consisted of blowing 50p on Refresher bars in the tuck shop and murdering Abba's 'Knowing Me Knowing You' in the class talent show. I came last.

There was no high school prom, either. Just a disco in the gym hall, where the static electricity caused by dancing to an Adam Ant song while wearing a taffeta puffball skirt almost resulted in spontaneous combustion of the thighs. Then I missed the half-time sandwiches because I was outside snogging my boyfriend, demonstrating potential sporting prowess should the Olympic Committee ever decide to introduce a new endurance event called the Prolonged Lip Lock.

However, the area in which I really feel cheated of celebratory activity is the whole pregnancy/baby period. I gave birth to my youngest eleven years ago. Back then, you announced you were pregnant and then there was a lull until the baby was born and everyone you've ever known appeared at the door clutching a box of Pampers and a selection of hand-knitted accoutrements.

These days, there's barely time to squeeze all the new traditions into a nine-month time frame.

The latest pregnancy celebratory occasion is the 'sex-reveal' party. In the old days, that term was more concerned with the conception, and was conducted by a kiss-and-tell opportunist in a Sunday newspaper.

Now it involves a large cake, with icing that is either blue or pink to announce the gender of the babe.

Hot on the booteed heels of that shindig comes the obligatory baby shower.

And in the name of Demi Moore's private bits, that's followed by the tastefully done 'naked and pregnant' pics. Sorry, I had to stop to shudder there at the thought of flashing my nuddy bod. If I have to follow in Demi's footsteps,

Party Popper

I'd rather opt for engaging Bruce Willis in my specialist event, the Prolonged Lip Lock.

But my biggest regret? Missing out on the best new tradition of all – The Push Present. Yep, apparently menfolk now stump up for a token of appreciation to reward new mammas for giving birth. As with most ridiculously indulgent trends, it was born on Planet Celebrity. Mariah Carey got diamond earrings. Nicole Kidman got a £100,000 necklace. Marc Anthony presented Jennifer Lopez with earrings that cost £2 million. Kanye West just lavished Kim Kardashian with a ring that cost over half a million quid. And it seems us commoners can at least expect the other half to do a quick trolley dash round H. Samuel.

Shallow it may be, but I'm seething with the injustice of missing out on a bit of bling.

Dear husband, I know we're eleven years down the line and that stable door is well and truly shut, but can I have a wee retrospective trinket please?

Just think of the positive impact that it would have on our lives. It would be a beautiful acknowledgement of that special day. It would be a fitting thanks for all that exertion. And I could shove it on eBay when we need to raise funds for the school prom helicopter. ◆

Love, Mum

Ladies, prepare to feel loved and special. This week we have a double whammy of appreciation – International Women's Day tomorrow and Mother's Day on Sunday. Which means that we will take the opportunity to study the highbrow issues affecting our gender, demand an end to inequality, commemorate our achievements, while leaving magazines in every room with the page open at an advert for a new face-cream that costs the same as a barrel of crude oil but promises you'll look like a supermodel by lunchtime.

Or is that just in this house?

I'll be celebrating tomorrow with my merry gang of chums by performing that traditional ritual of womanhood – congregating around my kitchen table with coffee, vino and several large bags of crisps shaped as bacon rashers, while analysing every detail of our lives since we did exactly the same thing last week. If we were penguins and David Attenborough was filming our gathering, he would no doubt observe the particularly loud cackle of mutual companionship (raucous laughter at the latest mortifying disaster). Also of note would be the tactile act of empathy (hug for anyone who has had a trauma/sadness/forgot to set the Sky+ for Grey's Anatomy). And there would be a detailed explanation of the gesture of solidarity in the face of attack (pursed lips and a harrumphing of the bosom when presented with a criticism of any of our pack or their brood).

Mamma penguins will then waddle off home to count down the hours until the one day of the year they are guaranteed to bask in a bubble of adoration.

Loosely translated, that means a cup of tea and a fried egg sandwich delivered to the duvet first thing in the morning, followed by a box of Quality Street and a bunch of daffodils liberated from the garden. Again, maybe just my house.

I truly appreciate the thought and the effort, but note to the Low brood, you really don't have to splash your pocket money on pressies or raid the flower beds. No, really. The truly special things in life are the ones that don't cost a penny. So my darling offspring, if you really want to spoil me on Sunday, here are my top ten suggestions for making my day blissful.

No-one is allowed to put anything in the washing basket all day. You may also hide the ironing pile and perhaps even tell me that all the ironing is up to date. I don't care if it's a lie – I'm happy to be humoured.

Announce that Low's taxi service has the day off as no-one requires a lift anywhere.

Go out with the statutory fiver for sports activities/water/ emergencies and – gasp – bring back change. Spring into action when this causes mother to faint.

Maintain bathroom in condition that does not require breathing equipment or a canary.

Cook lunch and dinner, without leaving the kitchen looking like it's been struck by a twister.

Swear on the holy Mother's Day card that no, you wouldn't rather have a Goddess-like, yummy mummy who does the school run in leather trousers and swishy shampoo-advert hair.

Agree to a moviefest of *Notting Hill*, *Love Actually* and *Bridget Jones's Diary* while proclaiming that the afore-mentioned are indeed cinematic classics.

Announce that you've thought long and hard about my priorities in life and now understand the importance I attach to handbags.

Do not screw up face and make retching sounds when mother expresses a wish to spend a long weekend on a tropical island with Daniel Craig.

And finally, most importantly, throw in hourly declarations of love and devotion.

Yes, there's a lot there to think about, but my sons, just remember it could be worse.

Have you heard about the face cream that's the same price as a barrel of crude oil? ◆

The Scream

It's a miracle I'm here.

To fully appreciate my frame of mind for the last week, picture my face. Now imagine it wide-eyed. Terrified. Mouth wide with screams. Now turn the page upside down.

That is the sight that greeted innocent bystanders last week when I took the kids on our impromptu Theme Park Tour of Britain.

Otherwise known as the week of 'Oh good grief my internal organs are not meant to dangle fifty feet in the air.'

I blame those merchants of all that is scary in this world:

My children.

I had to travel to London for a meeting on Monday. Obviously, this came with logistical considerations because at the moment I'm embarking on that stressful, hugely difficult task, up there with splitting the atom and developing space travel.

I'm trying to keep the kids occupied for six weeks of summer holidays during a staycation.

Yes, that sad, sun-deprived situation has dawned once more. I've decided to skip the annual holiday this year and pay off the credit cards instead.

That noise you can hear is my bank manager singing 'My Way' through a megaphone.

It almost makes me feel like a real grown-up. Next, I'll be buying a twin-set and pearls and thinking about pension plans.

Incidentally, who designed the word 'staycation' to sound like it was something relatively enjoyable?

It should be a frazzlecation. Stresscation. A houseworkation.

And don't tell the bloke with the megaphone, but I'm not sure the financial benefits are all they're cracked up to be, given that taking the boys to the cincma, with a pit stop for a hot dog and popcorn, costs approximately the same as a fortnight in the Maldives.

But back to my meeting.

The original plan was to sort out childcare and fly up and down in the same day, but after pondering the options I decided to take the car, the kids, and visit family in Leeds and London.

So far, so civilised.

Then Low the Younger interjected his words of wisdom.

At eleven, he is fairly convinced that he's twenty-five. I expect him to appear at any moment with application forms for the bureaucratic signs of adulthood – a job, a mortgage and a Matalan card.

The Scream

'But Mum, if we're going from Leeds to London, we could go the way that passes Alton Towers.'

Indeed. Damn you, Google Earth.

'And then, we could stop at Thorpe Park and Chessington World of Adventures too?'

No we couldn't. Definitely not. Absolutely no way. Those were the thoughts that went through my mind. Unfortunately, they were cancelled out by his hopeful wee face and general air of optimism.

I've been on many road trips in the past. A pal and I once did a Thelma and Louise from New York to Orlando, stopping on the way for an enraged wife to attempt to break our motel door down with an axe because she thought her husband was inside with a girlfriend. Never have I been so close to featuring in a *Crimewatch* reconstruction.

I once drove from Niagara Falls to Philadelphia, getting lost 5,465 times on the way.

Last year, the chums and I headed for Pitlochry, and braved the twin threats of motorway services tea and torrential rain.

But the Theme Park Tour of Britain?

I flew through the air. I screamed while my face was being G-forced to the consistency of marshmallow. I dangled. Yes, dangled from a structure that looked like it was only a few fitments up the technologically advanced scale from my whirligig.

And I prayed. I prayed to the Gods of Chunky Burds, not to let me fall out or get stuck.

Never again. Warn the bank manager next year I'm going off to faraway shores and I don't care what I have to do to afford to get there.

Or if all else fails – NASA, need any volunteers for that space travel? ◆

Baby Weight

I blame Victoria Beckham for many things. The pout. That ridiculous hand-on-hip, one-foot-forward photo pose now considered mandatory across the globe.

And the smugtastic fact that after each of her pregnancies she was back in the size-zero frock before the midwife had returned home from her shift, poured a cuppa and flicked over to the latest episode of *Holby City*.

She's not alone. Heidi Klum strutted her stuff on the Victoria's Secret catwalk just five weeks after giving birth to daughter Lou. Giselle was in a bikini the size of three tea bags shortly after entering the sleep-deprived realms of motherhood. And after welcoming the pitter patter of tiny feet, Jessica Alba swiftly eradicated a bulge no bigger than a family-size steak pie.

Thankfully, there's a new voice of reason on Planet Fame.

After the birth of daughter Lincoln (let's just skip right past the moniker) in March, actress Kristen Bell, thirty-three, has added a large dose of reality to the post-pregnancy diet debate, tweeting, 'I'm proud to sit out the baby weight rat race.'

Well, break out the bunting. I've yet to lose my baby weight and I probably should make it a priority now that my youngest is months old. 136 months old, to be exact. The only six-pack in my life comes from Golden Wonder and features a choice of Cheese and Onion, Salt and Vinegar or Ready Salted.

But, while I wholeheartedly concede that replacing the baby bump with the physique of someone about to give birth to an average-size panda is unhealthy, so too is the celebrity obsession with getting back into the size-six jeans an hour and a half after popping out a little Banana Boo Dixiebucket.

Last week, *OK!* magazine was forced to apologise to Wills and Kate after their front cover carried the headline, 'Kate's Post-Baby Weight Loss Regime.'

Seriously? When is the media going to stop obsessing over how long it takes a famous face to get back into her thong after delivering a small human being? Like Liz Hurley, Kim Kardashian West has gone into hiding, and hasn't been seen since the arrival of her little compass point. I'm fairly convinced she's in an underground bunker, wearing a sweat suit while strapped to a toning table, screeching 'squeeze me a guava juice.'

I'd bet my last black baggy T-shirt that she'll emerge in the next week or two, in a multi-million-dollar photo shoot, with a body that's sprung back into shape like a catapult.

Baby Weight

Yet I find it incredibly sad that those early weeks of bliss are overshadowed by a desperate need to regain the pre-preggers silhouette. When my sons were born, I ate well because I was breastfeeding and excelled in several sports: weight training (hauling out the wheelie bin), running (to the door to answer it lest the doorbell wake up the baby) and the 100 metres hurdles (that's one lap of the house while propelling buttocks over baby chairs, tables, changing bags and an ironing mountain so high it came with Sherpas and a base camp).

But I couldn't have been happier because my main concern was childcare, not calories.

Final word goes to Kristen. 'I'd like to get back down to where I was before the baby... But if this is where my body wants to be, so be it. I'm not going to make myself miserable for the rest of my life trying to get back to where I was before.'

Wise words. Little Lincoln might not grow up with a mother who's a size zero – but with a mum like that she's bound to grow up with a healthy waistline and an even healthier sense of perspective. ◆

Equal Measures

Blokes, no wonder you're confused. To be honest, I'm a tad perplexed myself.

When I was young, and chivalrous dinosaurs roamed the Earth, the rules of politeness were pretty straightforward. Hold a door open. Give a lady a seat. Walk on the road side of the pavement. Help a woman on with her coat.

Apparently, over the last few decades, someone has shifted the gallantry goalposts.

Seven months' pregnant Jo Swinson, our current equalities minister, put unisexknickers in a twist on both sides of the PC divide last week when she had to stand for twenty minutes during Prime Minister's Questions as no-one offered her a seat.

One of her team later suggested that to vacate a chair for a pregnant woman would be sexist – although Jo later retracted the sentiment. The sheer nonsense of this just compelled me to pause and sigh like a Jane Austen heroine in front of a large puddle.

Navigating the rules of equality is now more challenging than rewiring a plug with one hand.

In our post-millennium society, where does courtesy end and sexism start? And how is the next generation of men supposed to understand the nuances of gender politics?

I'm bringing up two boys who are about to hit the teenage years.

When they were small, basic manners were a priority: say 'please' and 'thank you'; don't interrupt when adults are speaking; ask to be excused from the table after eating dinner.

Not that it was always easy. When Low the Younger was a toddler, he developed a liking for the word okay, leading to a daily exchange of:

Me: 'Say "please".' Him: 'Okay.'

Me: 'No, not "OK", "please". You have to say "please" if you want something.'

Him: 'OK.'

Me: 'No, "please". Not "OK". Say "please".'

At which point I'd sigh wearily and pass over all my worldly goods to make it stop.

As they grew up, I added a few more requirements under the heading of Consideration For Others.

They've been taught that they should hold open a door for anyone coming behind them, and always offer their seat to a woman (pregnant or not) or an elderly person of either gender.

Incidentally, when it comes to a mother-to-be or anyone

born before me, I do the same. In the case of the former, it's empathy, in the case of the latter, it's the ghost of my no-nonsense granny ordering me to give up my seat or there'll be no 5p packet of Refreshers from the shops on the way home.

My sons also open the car door for me if they're there first, help me with heavy bags, and occasionally hold my Primark parka while I slide into it. Their dad has always done the same and I do appreciate it. It's nice. Kind. Thoughtful.

So, gents, be assured that some of us do still welcome common courtesy.

To those MPs who let a seven months' pregnant woman stand while they hogged the benches? Next time, get on your feet and have some manners.

And if that offends either side of the PC brigade, please feel free to report me.

I'd suggest a stern letter to the equalities minister. Hopefully, she'll be sitting down when she reads it. ◆

Party On

In times of real challenges facing our world – war, global financial chaos, Miley Cyrus's foam finger – I've absolutely no idea why the following story made national news. However, to take our minds off anything to do with horror, overdrafts or buttocks being shoogled in a provocative manner, I'm focusing on the headlines this week about an eighteen-year-old daughter of a Devon millionaire who threw an all-night jolly in her vast gardens, resulting in villagers up to six miles away making complaints to police.

A teenager throwing a slightly rowdy party? Well blow me down, Ethel, and pass me a Babycham.

It's shocking. Terrible. Outrageous.

As a responsible member of society I can assure you that I've never, ever done such a thing.

Erm, except the soirée that I threw when my parents were away that resulted in thirty sixteen-year-olds attempting to barbeque sausages at midnight. That was followed several hours later by the requirement to clean up a mass biohazard caused by thirty sixteen-year-olds with food poisoning.

Then there was the weekend that my parents returned a few hours earlier than planned and my brother was forced to distract them by pretending to faint in the front driveway, giving our pals time to escape out of the back windows. It was like the SAS storming of a building in reverse.

We even had a pre-party system. Parents out the door. Wait ten minutes. Fluff up the mullet, then put a Wham record on the stereo. Proceed to cover all furniture with old sheets, lock away cutlery and crockery, replace with packets of paper plates and plastic cups and nip to the shops for our nutritional needs: twenty-four packets of Skips, twenty-four packets of Monster Munch, six tins of custard and a loaf. Yes, man can live on custard, toast and artificially flavoured carbohydrate snacks.

Sing it with me… Club Tropicana, Skips are free.

In our defence, we never upset the neighbours, we all survived, and we rarely got caught, mainly because this all happened in prehistoric times before Facebook, the Internet and camera phones.

Not that I'll be admitting any of this to my sons now that they're on the cusp of teendom. Oh no. Mother was a halo and a certified miracle away from being a saint, boys. I spent the entire years from thirteen to eighteen studying the environmental effects of ozone layer damage and loitering around pedestrian crossings waiting to help old ladies across roads.

Party On

And only if that strategy doesn't work will I reluctantly 'fess up to the facts and present them with my diary of shame.

It will be called: Things Your Mother Did That You Must Not Repeat.

A fortnight in Benidorm with pals at seventeen. Should you break this rule, expect a large pot plant to be beside you at all times. Don't worry if it sneezes, that'll just be my hayfever.

Thoust shall not smoke or drink or claim to be at a sleepover when you and your neon green legwarmers are actually at an all-night disco.

Leaving home at sixteen will not be an option. You will stay until mother is ready to cut the apron strings. Thirty-five is a perfectly acceptable age to attain independence.

Do not map a future with an international star without thorough research. It took many years to recover from the realisation that the father of my children wouldn't be George Michael.

And, finally, the whole party thing? No matter how well you clean up, mother will know. The best you can hope for is that you come up with a sincere gesture of apology and compliments to soften the blow.

You might want to start with Wham's greatest hits. A bumper packet of Skips. And 'Mum, your mullet looked great.' ◆

Lucky Stars

If Clint Eastwood appeared at my door doing a survey to determine the number of punks feeling lucky, I'd simply introduce myself by my middle name, Jinx.

I have rubbish luck.

I've never won a raffle prize. Or the lottery. Or been in the right place at the right time. Instead, I plod along from one unexpected blip to another.

In the last few weeks, my roof leaked, my car broke down, my computer crashed, my phone smashed, my toaster blew up, I lost my purse, I fell over, I got two parking tickets, and last Thursday I dropped and decimated a packet of Hobnobs.

But there was a wee ray of exciting good fortune on the horizon.

I was flying to New York last Friday morning to work there all weekend on the novel I'm writing with my pal, Ross King, who's based in LA. We thought we'd meet halfway and do the final edit before we send it in to the publisher.

Lucky Stars

If you watch Ross on *Daybreak*, you'll know that – when he's not writing a novel – he's a regular jet-setter who zips around the globe, interviewing stars and inhabiting celebrity circles. Meanwhile, I'm a fairly knackered mother of two whose life has all the balance of Kylie Minogue and John McCririck on a see-saw.

My daily existence has no glamour. None. I sit at a laptop making up imaginary people for up to twelve hours a day, usually seven days a week. I wear trousers with elasticated waists. I spend every night and all weekend transporting the brood to their 4,529 sports and music activities.

And even though saying, 'I'm flying to New York for the weekend' sounds swanky, the reality was a little different. We'd booked an airport hotel, an hour outside Manhattan. The plan was to jump straight off the plane, work for forty-eight hours, back on plane, home. The closest I'd actually get to Manhattan was buying a postcard with the NYC skyline at the airport.

Still, in my usual stressed-out state, I was so looking forward to two relaxing plane journeys, movies each way and a read of a Jackie Collins. Bliss. Lucky me!

Turns out the Universe had other plans.

On Thursday afternoon, I collected Low the Younger from school and he was feeling unwell. Nauseous. Pain in stomach. Dreadful colour.

Despite being the queen of the overreaction, I stayed calm, wrapped him up in bed, inclined to think it was the bug that's doing the rounds. Within an hour or so, I knew it wasn't.

The wee soul was doubled up in pain, vomiting, clutching the right side of his abdomen. We hurtled up to the A&E at the RAH in Paisley to have him checked out. The doctors and nurses were excellent and seven hours later, at 1 a.m., he was transferred by ambulance to Yorkhill, as there was a possibility that surgery would be required. When we arrived, the medical staff there examined him and decided to hold off until morning. It was the right decision. Over the next couple of days, it became clear that it wasn't the original suspected diagnosis of appendicitis, but a virus that had caused glands in his abdomen to become inflamed and swollen.

I never did get to New York and I didn't care in the least. Because after spending time in a children's hospital surrounded by sick children, with anxious parents sleeping beside them, holding hands across the beds, you realise that nothing else matters.

Unlucky? Absolutely not.

Low the Younger is fine. We left the hospital, said goodbye to all the fantastic medical staff, the lovely parents and brilliant kids.

And I took my boy home.

That's how lucky we are. ◆

Teen Spirit

I don't know how it happened. One minute I was being wheeled out of the maternity ward clutching a plate of toast and a little blue bundle, and now, in the blink of an eye, he's almost an adult.

Low the Elder turned thirteen this week. Thirteen. That's a Gillette Easy Shave and a splash of Paco Rabanne away from manhood.

In five years he'll be old enough to drink. In four years he'll be old enough to drive. In three years he'll be old enough to get married. Not that he'll be allowed to go anywhere near an aisle with a blushing bride at the end. I've spent many years teaching him that marriage should be delayed until he's in his forties, and even then, only if he comes home to his mother for weekends.

In the meantime, the dawning of the teen years means I'm going to have to loosen the maternal strings, a thought that makes my parenting panic button twerk like Miley Cyrus on Red Bull.

My name is Shari Low and I'm an overbearing mother.

I'm not proud. Although, to be fair, as he pushes against the barriers of childhood, the fact that I'm at the other side of the wall knocking up steel reinforcements isn't exactly a newsflash.

The night he was born, we stood at the window of the RAH in Paisley at 3 a.m. looking at the stars, only for the perfect peace to be interrupted by wailing ambulances bringing in intoxicated post-club revellers.

'That'll never be you in there,' I whispered. 'Because when you're old enough to go to clubs, I'll take you there, and I'll wave you off... and then I'll be sitting outside with a flask and sandwiches until you need a lift home again.'

As he grew, I loved the kiddiedom years. I adored those sticky fingered, squashed banana days when they didn't want to go anywhere without you and the sun only shone if you were there, preferably clutching a *Barney* DVD, a football and a ten pence mixture from the corner shop.

I used to be the first person he came to with his worries. The last person he wanted to speak to at night. His whole wide world.

Now I'm the one deploying interrogation tactics to ascertain his movements and withholding pocket money until I can enter his room without an advance party armed with Febreze.

It's only a matter of time before he starts avoiding my calls, blanking my texts and leaving my emails unopened. Look, the Manual of Motherhood doesn't actually state where maternal devotion ends and stalking starts.

Sadly, the seeds of rebellion and intolerance have already taken root. He's doing that thing they teach in man school, the instinctive reaction to everything from over-protectiveness to demands to know every detail of his schedule from now until the end of the decade.

Yes, he's started to roll his eyes. Followed, occasionally, by the weary shake of the head.

Sob.

However, it's a small consolation to know that overbearing motherhood is a global issue.

I recently read an article about a new American dating website where mothers choose potential girlfriends for their sons. Of course, it's ridiculous. Pathetic. Completely suffocating and worryingly indicative of control issues on the part of the mother. And for anyone interested, I plan to have www.yermumpicksyergirlfriend.com up and running within the month.

And to that special person I one day choose and grant access to my darling forty-year-old son, I can only say this…

Love him as much as I do.

Give him freedom and space to breathe.

And good luck with the mother-in-law. ◆

Good Intentions and Parenting Inventions ››››

Happy New Year

Happy New Year! How's the head? How's the waistline? And the house?

I'm fine on the first count, but as for the second and the third, if those nice chaps at Hoover or Dyson would like to pop round and test their latest products on my carpets, I'd be much obliged. Just ignore me as I lie under a withering festive tree, in stretchy trousers, attempting to recover from an overdose of the big purple ones out of the Quality Street box.

I had planned to be sickeningly optimistic and make today's column all about my resolutions for 2014, but let's face it, there's as much chance of me sticking to a New Year vow as there is of having Bradley Cooper's love child. Although Bradley, if you read this and you're partial to a chick in leggings, emitting a faint aroma of hazelnuts and caramel, you know where to find me.

Last year's aspirations went downhill quicker than an Olympic toboggan.

Because I Said So

As with every year, I resolved to lose weight, get fit, refrain from embarrassing my children, cease worrying, quash my chronic hypochondria, clear the credit cards and stop buying clothes that don't fit me in the hope that I'll 'slim into them'.

Oh, and I was determined that my work/life balance would no longer have all the stability of Liam and Noel Gallagher having a square go while balancing on a skateboard.

I had this vision of a serene, calm, organised woman who sailed through life being smug and super-controlled, taking time out for herself and achieving her aims and goals while sporting perfectly coiffured hair and thighs that could crack nuts.

Unfortunately, reality painted a slightly different picture. Like every year in recent memory 2013 consisted mostly of days of frantic rushing, followed by attempts to rustle up an edible meal in the ten minutes between work and kick-starting the night shift on Mum's Taxis, while fretting over a deadline and worrying that my tickly cough could be dengue fever.

Low the Elder (thirteen) decided that next time I start a Mexican wave at one of his sporting events, he's leaving home. And eleven-year-old Low the Younger announced he's spending his Christmas vouchers on a barge pole to stop me committing the horrific crime of spontaneously hugging him in front of his pals.

I'm using the size 14 PVC trousers I recently bought on eBay as a draught excluder, because I'm still a size 18/20 despite the fact that I've spent the last year on the 5:2 diet. However, I do concede that I continue to adapt it to suit my nutritional needs. For example, in December, every five After Eights were punctuated by two sticks of orange Matchmakers.

My fitness campaign has been similarly sporadic. In the last week, it has consisted of daily lunges... for the remote control. In the few hours I've taken off chasing a January deadline on my next novel, I've valiantly wrestled the remote from the hands of the sports-loving males in this house and used it to flick over to my trusty stock of Richard Curtis romcoms.

So this year I'm breaking the cycle of 'hope, fail, hope, fail, hope, fail' and going for acceptance.

I concede that I'll never be that organised, paragon of perfection, so my vow in 2014 is to have no resolutions whatsoever. None. I'm going to see what every day brings, cope with the rubbish bits and celebrate the good stuff.

And if I come across one of those serene, calm, organised people who sail through life being smug and super-controlled while sporting perfectly coiffured hair and thighs that could crack nuts...

Dear Low the Younger, any chance of borrowing your barge pole? ◆

Nappy Times

Congratulations to Simon Cowell. It's been incredible to see him with a new addition who is demanding, attention-seeking, makes a lot of noise without actually saying much, does nothing particularly interesting and requires regular incessant mollycoddling.

But now that he has a baby, he obviously won't be able to spend as much time with Nicole Scherzinger.

The photos with baby Eric are gorgeous, and the pop mogul has been waxing lyrical on new fatherhood.

However, I can't help thinking that he will perhaps look back on some of his recent assertions and revise his opinions.

The first questionable claim? Simon said: 'I never have and never will change a nappy.'

He may reconsider, the first time he's alone with the child and caught in an explosive situation after a meal of puréed carrot and spinach. Oh, and his theory that having a baby won't change his life too much? Good luck with that.

Nappy Times

Obviously, with an army of nannies and Sinitta always within hollering distance (note to self: send headphones for baby), Simon's experience of new fatherhood might not be typical of most.

But Si, for what it's worth, here are some of the things I learned after becoming a parent.

1. It's best to take one day at a time, be objective and maintain realistic expectations.

     But your child is the most handsome in the whole world and, yes, he/she will be the first professional sports-playing prime minister that ever cured diseases before going on to pilot his/her own rocket into space.

2. As a parent, you are a sensible, reasonable person who doesn't overreact – unless the baby has a slight temperature in which case the emergency services, the World Health Organization and the head of the NHS should be alerted immediately.

3. You will never wear white again.

4. There are 3,452 ways to purée food. They all look like gunk.

5. No matter where in a room a child splats a spoon, the food will end up on something that's dry-clean only.

     And remember how you mocked other parents for that really annoying thing of making plane noises when trying to encourage their child to eat?

By month 10, you will have better landing patterns than air traffic control.

6. You will love your friends' children even more if they behave worse than yours in public.

7. You used to be capable of conducting a deep, informed discussion about international politics and the effects of global climate change.

    Now you'll have three-hour chats about baby body functions.

8. A girl's best friend is a diamond. A parent's best friend is the washing machine.

9. Some mothers find it difficult if their partner comments on post-birth weight loss, given that said partner hasn't shot a melon out of part of his nether-located anatomy.

10. You will make comprehensive plans to shower, travel, sleep, socialise – and although the baby seems to be having no reaction, it's laughing inside.

11. The baby weight endures. From personal experience, this can last until the child is a teenager.

12. The dozens of items of baby equipment you bought? You'll only actually use four.

13. You know those soft-play areas that you always viewed as noisy and crowded? You'll realise they are designed by the Gods Of Give Me Five Minutes To Read The Papers And Have A Scone.

Nappy Times

Finally, just remember that, rich or poor, there are three golden rules:

- You can never give a baby too much love.
- Just do the best you can.
- And don't take the shift straight after the meal of puréed carrot and spinach. ◆

The Ring

There are many ground-breaking things I wish for in this world. Cures for all diseases. A space vehicle that will transport the current government to a galactic black hole. Calorie-free banoffee pie.

So I was a tad disappointed when I read about the latest breakthrough on Planet Science. It's called The Ring. Yep, jewellery.

In fairness, it's a special ring that can do spectacular stuff. Slip it on your finger and this invention can switch on lights and control household appliances just by wagging your finger in mid-air. It can write emails, send texts and answer calls. It plays music, pays bills and organises your day.

I'm sure it's a truly revolutionary piece of kit and big cheers to the very smart people who invented it.

But am I excited?

Alas, no.

Because, you see, I can already do all of those things.

The Ring

So techie bods, if you're listening, I'd like a middle-aged mother variety. Just so we're clear, that doesn't mean I want it to come with a box set of *Revenge* and a nostalgia for Duran Duran hits.

It just needs to be able to take over some of the motherhood tasks that I currently find insurmountable.

I'll retain all the wonderful bits of parenthood. I'll keep the laughs and the dancing in the kitchen. I'll remain responsible for the holidays and the snuggling up on the couch to watch a movie. I'll continue to treasure the moments when they tell you about their day and the love that goes both ways.

But there are some areas where I need the intervention of science.

Let's start with the basics. It would be great if the Ring of Motherhood could do the housework, iron the uniforms and put the toilet seat down.

Next, we ramp up the difficulty scale to a level that's close to splitting the atom.

Dear ring, please take over all morning duties.

This involves a system of vocal commands that ascends both in volume and panic, and goes something like:

'Morning! Time to get up, my lovelies.'

'Come on, darlings, your breakfast is on the table.'

'Boys, you're going to be late if you don't get up right now!'

'GET OUT OF YOUR BEDS!!!!!!'

Approximately forty-five minutes later, this should be followed by another pre-programmed set of commands.

'Right, darlings, let's get to the car.'

'Come on boys, we need to go right now.'

'Boys, quick as you can. What do you mean you can't find your PE kit?'

'ANYONE WHO ISN'T IN THE CAR IN TEN SECONDS IS GROUNDED FOR A MONTH!'

The Ring should then deal with the standard school run irritants by spotting drivers blocking roads and parking on corners and yelling, 'No you can't bloody stop there because it's dangerous, you twonk!'

The next shift comes at dinner time.

'What's for tea, Mum?'

'Not sure yet. What would you like?'

'Dunno. What is there?'

At this point, The Ring rhymes off every single thing in the fridge, freezer and cupboard.

It locates a secret pile of change when you realise you forgot to go to the bank so there's no cash for dinner money, bus fares, school trips.

It comes to the rescue when the child announces that they need a wizard/king/kangaroo costume. By tomorrow.

In the cinema, it blocks mobile phones, so that the inconsiderate git behind you can't answer calls halfway through *Despicable Me 2*.

And finally, it delivers a reverse of the wake-up procedures to get them to bed at night.

Now that's an invention to get excited about.

The Ring

And no pressure, but it's only three weeks until Mother's Day and I'd like it for then. If not, I'll go for the second best thing.

Please alert my children as to where to attain the Duran Duran CD and the calorie-free banoffee pie. ✦

Supermum

Happy Mother's Day! Yes, I know I'm early, but I thought I'd provide a wee reminder that could be left open in prominent places to let your loved ones know it's time to splash out on the Quality Street.

Not that I'm materialistic and shallow. Actually, I am. In my opinion, nothing says 'I love you' quite like a River Island voucher and a Terry's Chocolate Orange.

However, this year I honestly don't care about pressies because I'm just thankful my offspring are still talking to me.

I'm afraid the last twelve months have been a time of reckoning in Chez Low.

My two wee guys used to think I was infallible, invincible, knew everything and always did the right thing. I was like their very own superhero. Yep, I was Supermum, with powers that included being able to predict the future (if the wind changes your face will stay like that), stop chaos by raising my mighty right eyebrow of warning and solve all traumas with the fearless combination of cuddles and Jaffa Cakes.

Supermum

Now, that time has passed. My sons are eleven and thirteen and my maternal tall tales are coming back to haunt me.

Two incidents brought it home this week. Low the Younger is studying World War II in school and came home outraged. 'Mum, you used to tell me that carrots made us see in the dark. Do you know that's a lie?' Apparently, that pesky education thing had taught him that the carrot myth originated in a wartime propaganda campaign. It's true. I looked it up.

The second blip was caused by a more recent development. A new species of deep-water fish has been discovered which has four eyes, giving it 360-degree vision. I suggest we call it the Mother Fish, given that I always told my children I had eyes in the back of my head. Score two, for the Supermum lie detector.

Shamefully, the porkies are nothing new. There's the whole Santa thing. He may be real, but come on, it's ridiculous to tell children that he's only got nine reindeers. I count at least thirteen. Dasher, Dancer, Prancer, Vixen, Comet, Cupid, Donner, Blitzen, Rudolph, Argos, eBay, Visa and Mastercard.

The Tooth Fairy and the Easter Bunny have a lot to answer for, too.

I blame my granny for starting the lies. She swore that if I ate my crusts, my hair would go curly. It remained poker straight, aside from an Eighties flirtation with a perm/mullet combo that made me look like Andy Murray. On a bad hair day. In a wind tunnel.

It's not just my big fat fibs that have been exposed – welcome to the era of 'do as I say, not as I do'.

Raising my boys, I emphasised the importance of being motivated and committed. 'See things through and don't give up until you succeed,' I'd witter.

They've now watched me start and fail countless new diets and exercise regimes and abandon the ironing in favour of a lie-down with the latest Marian Keyes.

I drill them in the need to focus on homework and ignore distractions. Then the doorbell rings and I take an hour off work to have a chat to my pals.

I teach them about saving and the importance of sensible spending – until my credit card bill cracks a floor tile when it thuds through the letterbox.

I've always told them they must never be shallow or materialistic.

Pot. Kettle. Woe.

Yes, Supermum has been unmasked as a fraud.

I can only hope they don't follow in my footsteps and that they realise the lies and hypocritical lessons were all for their own good.

And if they don't?

At least I'll be able to bribe them with a River Island voucher and a Terry's Chocolate Orange. ◆

Not Guilty

If it were a multiple choice quiz question, it would go something like this: Name the emotion commonly experienced when raising children, that is exacerbated in times of junk food, school holidays and the secret loathing of concerts involving small kids and recorders. Is it:

A. Giddy bliss

B. Deep fulfilment

C. Guilt

Read me my rights, officer.

However, this week, only thirteen per cent of working mothers said they felt guilty about being away from their children, compelling Mumsnet chief exec Justine Roberts to say, 'Perhaps it's time to banish the cliché of the guilty working mum once and for all.'

I'm all for jumping on the guilt-free bus, but sadly, I've yet to meet another mum who hasn't felt a twinge of self-reproach at some point in the parenting process.

Mine started early. Oh, the plans I had when I was pregnant. My children would have a diet of organic goodness, they would only watch TV if it was an educational documentary on nuclear physics, and we'd spend every day in a cake-baking, flower-pressing, language-learning, healthy eating bubble of parental perfection.

Cue reality.

I'm lucky enough to have a job that I can do at home, and I'd like to thank Barney the Dinosaur for providing years of emergency childcare. And guilt.

Then there were the many occasions that I contemplated dressing the Low clan in a spy-like disguise when entering fast-food joints (chicken burgers, fresh orange and a fruit bag) to avoid being spotted and judged by the families who never left home without a stash of homemade rice cakes. Guilt.

My children are indeed bilingual. But they only speak English and Glaswegian. Guilt.

On long car journeys we'd start off with jolly songs and upbeat games of I Spy.

I spy with my little eye something beginning with C. Cars. Or T. Trucks. Sometimes B. Bus. After the 345th 'Are we there yet?' I'd cave and crack open the portable DVD player and a box set of *Bob the Builder*. And guilt.

Every year when the school holidays were looming, I'd have visions of giving my sons 100 per cent of my time, recreating the idyllic, action-packed breaks experienced by those perfect families who wear matching jumpers while cycling through the countryside in adverts for holiday camps and probiotic drinks.

Then life would interfere and suddenly the days would become a chaotic balance of fun, games, footie in the garden, and more afternoons whence my large purple friend kept two energetic wee boys amused while I typed up 5,000 words of the next novel.

But, oh, the guilt.

Except… the boys are twelve and thirteen now and they're two happy, well-balanced individuals who seem to have survived my overstretched parenting fails without turning into delinquents. Or junk-food addicts. And I don't need a crowbar to get them off the sofa or therapy to wean them off reruns of *Storage Wars*.

In fact, as I write this, they're both indulging in their favourite pastimes. My bookworm is lying on the couch with the new Robert Muchamore, and his brother is at a basketball court, where he's been training for hours.

Apparently, that makes this – according to both of them – 'a brilliant holiday'.

So, I'm giving up with the grand plans that leave me crushed when they don't come off. I'm abandoning the dreams of being that family wearing matching jumpers on their bikes. I'm quashing the feeling that I'm somehow short-changing them by juggling work/family/house/movie channel.

Instead, I'm agreeing with Justine – it's time to banish the negativity and self-doubt.

No more guilt.

Although, it does leave one less option when we're playing car games.

No more 'I spy with my little eye, something beginning with G.' ◆

Confessions of a Competitive Mum

Okay, here goes. It's time to step forward and admit the truth. I'm shrugging off the shame. I'm going to be loud, proud and I may even start a Mexican wave.

My name is Shari Low. And I'm a competitive mum.

This week, the queen of our movement, Judy Murray, spoke up to defend fellow members of our much-scorned and derided gang saying, 'There's something about being a competitive mum, especially when the children are male. If I were the dad of sons, I wouldn't have been noticed.'

She's right. And as a fellow MASK (Mother of A Sporty Kid), I'm aware of just how easy it is to be pulled into the feverish grip of sporting hyperactivity. Please note that this exertion applies only to spectating and not on-field participation. The last time I took part in a team sport I was sixteen, and half-time consisted of oranges, water, and snogging my boyfriend round the back of the changing rooms.

When I started writing this column, my sons were one and

three. In the primary school years I'd roar my encouragement at sports day, but it was just in fun as I had no competitive edge whatsoever. Which is just as well, as Low the Elder was highly talented in the sporting field of mud-diving while Low the Younger demonstrated a particular aptitude in the little-known challenge of Wotsit Consumption.

At school sports days I'd mock the mothers who'd sulk when their wee Usain Bolt didn't triumph when carrying an egg on school dinner cutlery. I'd take another bite of a white chocolate Magnum and gently roll my eyes at the mums that showed up in Lycra ready to trounce the opposition in the mother's race.

In the non-sports arena, I was equally as laid-back. Didn't get the lead role in the nativity? Don't worry, darling, the second sheep on the left played a vital role in the early years of Christianity.

As the years passed, my boys joined football teams and I'd duly show up, but to be honest, it was an excuse to hang out for an hour on the touchlines with the fellow MASKs and discuss vital sporting issues. Like the wardrobe choices of high-profile WAGs and David Beckham's ad campaigns for his new kecks.

Fast forward ten years and it all changed when – drum rolls, trumpets and a toot on a claxon – Low the Elder discovered basketball. When he started I was clueless. As far as I was concerned, an in-depth strategy was 'catch ball, put in round thing that's dangling on the wall'.

Then something happened. I had an out-of-body experience. He scored a basket in a crucial game and I was out of my seat, punching the air and yelling, 'Touch-down!'

I clearly hadn't grasped the sport-specific terminology.

Maybe it's admiration for how hard he trains. Perhaps I've just discovered a sport I actually love to watch. But ever since then, I've been a woman possessed. I cheer. I holler. I once leapt up to celebrate a win and pulled a hamstring. And – please don't judge me – I possess, oh the shame, a foam finger. Although I will add that it has never been used in a Miley-esque fashion.

And now the unthinkable has happened. My youngest has joined his brother on the b-ball court. See? I'm like, pure down with the lingo now.

However, if Judy's unapologetic, then so am I. I'm a competitive mother and I don't care. I'm going to wear my over-excitability like a badge of honour.

And to those laid-back mothers who think I'm ridiculous? Here lies a cautionary tale. Once upon a time, the chilled-out mum of the second sheep on the left discovered that it's a very swift, unexpected and painful leap from Wotsits to wiggling a foam finger. ✦

School's Moving On Up

It seems like only yesterday he marched to the school gate for the first time. There were tears. Snot. Wails. But once I got a grip of myself, I waved my five-year-old son off as he sauntered in for his first day of school. I said a silent prayer that he'd make friends. I fervently hoped he wouldn't be scared. And I seriously wondered if the weight of a backpack that was taller than him would make him topple over like an upturned turtle.

Fast forward seven years, and this week he strode into his primary school leaving dance while trying to ignore the fact that his mother had exactly the same expression she gets when someone dies at the end of *Casualty* – watery eyes and a petted lip that trembles like an emotionally overwrought guppy fish.

Friends, there's a new entry in the Little Book of Parental Sighs: That moment when your youngest child leaves primary school and you realise he's just a few years away from Pot Noodles and living in a bedsit with fourteen student pals.

Sob.

Prior to that tear-jerking, lump-in-throat moment, I'd only considered the plus sides of the situation. No more doing double school runs, now that Low the Younger will be joining his older brother at the big school. No more requirements for me to rustle up 200 woefully inferior fairy cakes for the Christmas party. No more getting up in the morning to those dreaded words, 'Mum, I need a crocodile/snowman/Scooby Doo costume for school today.'

I'm glad he's maturing and moving on to exciting stuff. I just hadn't realised it would come with such an emotional sucker-punch and a deafening snip of yet another apron string being cut.

Speaking from experience, I know what's ahead of me. Been there, done that, got the T-shirt that says 'My Kids Love Me – but only if their mates aren't around'.

If my youngest follows in the size eleven footsteps (yip, size eleven – I'm applying for a lottery grant to keep him in trainers) of his thirteen-year-old brother, the changes will be subtle at first. He'll no longer give me a kiss when I drop him off in the morning. He'll see me coming, and immediately go to Defcon One, in case I say or do anything that will cause him embarrassment in front of his chums. And then there's that physical act that they teach right before assembly on the first day in high school. The adolescent eye roll.

It's a one-stop gesture, applicable in all instances in which a mother makes gentle reprimands, helpful suggestions, bad jokes, hoovering requests and mutterings involving the words 'because I said so'.

Right now, my youngest still thinks I know stuff. In approximately six weeks and one day he'll decide I know nothing at all.

The irony doesn't escape me. I've always encouraged them to be independent. To think for themselves. They've been taught to cook, to budget, to keep their rooms on the non-biohazard side of toxic waste.

I'm just not ready for the increase in emotional independence that goes with it.

Look, I'm a mother. Double standards come with the territory.

So, Low the Younger, I'm happy for you, I really am. But you'll just have to bear with me as I tackle that difficult transition to the next stage of your education.

And in the meantime, just like my primary school graduate, I need to take what I've learned over the last few years, and put it in my skill bank in case I need it in the future. If anyone needs help to rustle up a crocodile/snowman/Scooby Doo outfit in an hour and a half, give me a shout. ◆

Uniform Smugdom

Another week, another new entry in my Big Book of Motherly Mishaps.

Every year I get caught up in the back-to-school frenzy that results in a panicked trolley dash round Marks & Spencer five minutes before the shop shuts on the night before the first bell of the new term rings.

Not this year. I was on the case.

In the first week of summer I bought full uniforms for both my boys and had them pressed, hung in the wardrobes and ready to go.

Oh the heart-swelling pride and smugness as I spent the next month planning my acceptance speech for my Mother of the Year award and gazing pitifully on my chums as they fell to their knees, wailing at the prospect of doing the uniform shop at the last minute.

'Och, I've already done it all,' I volunteered on several occasions, failing to disguise my overwhelming self-satisfaction.

'Maybe you should try getting organised early next year, too.'

I'm not sure on the exact wording of their replies but they came through gritted teeth and there may have been suggestions that ended with the word 'off'.

I didn't care. Nothing could dent my moment of triumph. Until…

Fast forward to the traumatic moment, only a few days ago, when my thirteen-year-old wandered into the kitchen and uttered a casual, 'Mum, I just tried on my new school trousers again. They don't fit me.'

What? Of course they fitted. I'd checked. I'd ironed them. I'd hung them up.

I was mother of the flipping year! He'd obviously tried on his wee brother's by mistake. Easily done. I sent him back for a second fitting and he appeared wearing a set of trews that looked absolutely fine – if Capri pants ever become standard uniform.

I could see the bones in his ankles. Sorry, had to stop there and take deep breaths until the fraught flashback subsided.

As the hems dangled, looking like flags at half-mast, reality dawned.

He's grown more than two inches in the summer holidays.

Another horrific thought dropped. 'Go try on your new school shoes,' I gasped dramatically, in the voice they use in movies when the mother is sending the hero off to risk his life in order to save civilisation.

Uniform Smugdom

He hobbled back through, his facial expression confirming his mutters of 'too small'.

In four weeks, his feet have gone from a size eleven to a size twelve. At age thirteen.

I wailed, while Flipper Low shrugged, missing the gravity of the situation entirely. I couldn't take the uniforms back because I'd already removed the tags. Size twelve school shoes are not exactly easy to find, and I now had approximately a day and a half to completely kit him out from head to exceptionally large toes.

And it's not as if I've got anything else on this week.

In an act of stupendous planning, my new novel, *Taking Hollywood*, comes out in the same week as my boys go back to school.

Every day is spent doing interviews in which I'm supposed to be all 'Jackie Collins', wafting around looking glamorous and dropping in dramatic and exciting anecdotes about my fascinating life.

Sigh. Who am I kidding? In reality, even on a good day, I'm a bit more Phil Collins in the glamour stakes. And those dramatic, exciting anecdotes?

Have you heard the one about the frantic mother doing a panicked trolley dash round Marks & Spencer five minutes before the shop shuts on the night before the first day of the new term? ◆

Can You... Stay Forever?

Parents – if the kids are within eyeshot of this page, distract them now. The shock of the fact I'm about to reveal could be too much. Nope, it's not about Santa. Or the Tooth Fairy. Or a change of wind leaving the face in a permanent scowl.

It's much more chilling. New research has brought to light a disturbing fact of modern family life – more than half of parents admit that they can't wait until their offspring leave home.

If I'm being perfectly candid, I can see the obvious advantage. As the mother of twelve- and thirteen-year-old boys, I long for the day when I don't utter 3,422 repetitions of sentences that start with, 'Can you...'

'Can you pick your clothes up off the floor?'

'Can you put your plates into that mysterious contraption sometimes referred to as a dishwasher?'

'Can you dig out my hazmat suit so I can wash your PE kit?'

But the other reasons cited in the study had me more confused than my husband in the soft furnishings area of IKEA.

Some parents wanted to turn the kids' bedroom into a gym. The very thought of that is enough to have me reaching for a cup of tea and a four-finger Kit Kat.

Forty-seven per cent said they wanted to take more romantic holidays as a couple. Well, strike that one. On hols, my kids aren't encumbrances, they're chief conspirators ('You distract Dad while I buy a lilo in the shape of a crocodile'). They also provide a vital divorce-avoidance service for a laid-back husband, and a wife who has the attention span of an over-caffeinated mosquito. My sons are happy to play basketball, swim, wrestle a crocodile-shaped lilo and listen to me murdering *The Shoop Shoop Song* on the karaoke while my dearly beloved reads in the sun and pretends not to know us.

Another popular reason for shoving the chicks out the nest is that the parental birds want their home to themselves. Hang on till I go bolt the doors. Who would make me laugh? Who would tell me my kitchen dancing is a pure beamer? Who would I bribe to watch superhero flicks that I really should have grown out of by now?

However, my prevailing motivation for tying the apron strings to the kids? The sad truth is that husband and I are not to be trusted on our own.

Before we had children, we were dedicated party people,

but thirteen years of responsibility and not getting out much has changed all that. Last weekend we discovered it's a latent force, waiting to resurface.

We had one rare night away. One night. We went out on the town, partied until dawn and then woke up painfully aware that we're no longer twenty-something wild ones who can swing their stuff into the small hours.

My head ached, my throat hurt and I'm fairly sure I now require a hip replacement. It took until Tuesday for my full cognitive abilities to return.

Should the kids leave home, I suspect it would be a slippery slope that ends with them getting phone calls from us at 4 a.m., begging them to collect us from a club and stop off on the way home for a kebab.

Clearly, we need the demands of parenthood to keep us out of trouble. So boys, I'm issuing a new request.

Can you pick up your clothes? Can you stack the dishwasher? And can you please live at home until middle age? ◆

Opening Arguments

Sometimes the punchlines just write themselves.

Picture the scene. I'm sitting in my kitchen and thirteen-year-old Low the Elder totters in from school, utters a quick 'Hey Mum' before divesting himself of a backpack that's big enough to contain a human body. He heads for the fridge, and only when he's armed with a sandwich in one hand and a drink in the other, does he regain the power of conversation.

'Listen to this,' I say chirpily, holding up the *Daily Record* and pointing to an article I've just been reading.

'A new study has discovered that children are more likely to argue with their mums than their dads.'

I could have been wearing a balaclava backwards and I'd still have seen his reply coming.

'No they don't,' he argued.

He was onto his crusts by the time I'd stopped laughing.

Still, I think I prefer my surveys when they have no basis in reality.

Give me something ridiculous like 'ninety-seven per cent of women would give up sex with Channing Tatum for a box of banana muffins' and I'll chuckle while rolling my eyes in a cynical fashion.

But this one dinged a bell of familiarity because, in this house, it's absolutely true. I love my boys. They're my very favourite people in the whole wide world, and most of the time this abode is filled with happiness and hilarity.

But there's absolutely no arguing with the fact that I'm higher up the bicker scale than their dad.

It doesn't take an MI6 investigation to establish mitigating evidence as to why this is the case.

For a start, I'm responsible for getting two adolescents from the depths of their duvets to school every morning, a task that brings more potential flash points than a pavement of paparazzi.

As husband toddles to work, clutching the newspaper and the second cappuccino of the day, he's totally oblivious to the fact that Low the Younger has just announced he's lost his school tie, needs a tenner, has forgot to do his science project, and can we build a space shuttle from a Shreddies box by 9 a.m.?

Then there are the housework disputes. The boys have weekly chores, with top of the list being that they have to keep their rooms clean and tidy. I raise concerns (translated from mum-speak as 'moan the face off them') when their bedroom starts to look like it's been ransacked. Husband would only notice the state of the firstborn's sleeping habitat if the council appeared and declared it an official landfill site.

In the same vein, 'house litter' twangs my feather duster. Why are there socks on the coffee table? Towels on the bathroom floor? And yes, my beloved child, I too think it's an outrage that modern technology has yet to invent plates that jump into the dishwasher all by themselves.

Finally, despite the fact that my cooking skills are up there with my ability to spin hula hoops on my bosoms, I'm usually on dinner duty, dealing with the inevitable, 'But why can't we all have different meals?' debate. Because you can't. End of story. Now eat your spaghetti Bolognese and pretend not to notice that it has the consistency of sludge.

Woe.

Thankfully, there's a wee ray of sunshine in the storm clouds, as the same survey concluded that while mums and children might argue more, she's also the first person they turn to when they have a problem.

So boys, I'm sorry that we occasionally encounter turbulence in our harmonious relationship, but I hope the fact that I'm always ready to listen to you balances out the conflict zones.

Always remember that, if you need to talk, I'm right here. But any chance you can tidy your landfill site first? ◆

Tinsel and Teenagers

I want to lodge a complaint with the Christmas Association of Parents' Advent, Nativity, Tinsel & Santa. Or Crimbo PANTS for short.

When I had my children, I thought I was in for sixteen merry years of festive over-celebration.

But no. Sob. No-one warned me that, as the children get older, some of the best yuletide moments get lost along the way.

Now that my boys are twelve and fourteen, there are so many challenging changes that I could do with a self-help book in the Secret Santa.

First up, the curtain has come down on the annual nativity play. Sorry, I had to pause there to recover from an emotional flashback to the unforgettable year Low the Younger reached his theatrical peak and played that famous biblical character, Humph the Camel.

When my elves were little, we'd spend a whole weekend decorating the house and they'd side with me in the annual

Tinsel and Teenagers

Low household dispute over the infamous singing penguins that belt out *We Wish You A Merry Christmas* every time someone passes them. By the time the Arctic birds have been on display for a week, the husband has usually delivered his annual, 'It's them or me,' ultimatum. At the moment, they're still on the sideboard, but he keeps glancing at them in the manner of a man with a dastardly plan.

Back then, my Low elves loved those performing creatures. This week, I caught them removing the batteries and putting them in their Xbox controller.

On Christmas Day, I cherished that moment at 5.30 a.m., when my superheroes would charge into our room – one dressed as Spiderman, the other wearing a Darth Vader cloak and helmet. That was our eldest. We did worry that we'd have to spend many years making excuses for the fact he preferred life on the dark side. He's wiped out civilisation and covered Earth in an impenetrable force field? Sorry about that. He may have had too many E-numbers as a child.

But back to the point. After dragging two parental zombies downstairs, they'd screech with delight and gratitude at every gift, and Christmas Day would pass in a flurry of joy and laughter.

I loved every minute of it and I treasure the memories, because now they're teenagers it's just not the same.

The days of the fun toys have gone and, on Christmas Day, I can't get them out of bed before 10 a.m. I consider this a near-criminal waste of at least four hours of Jenga time.

Because I Said So

When I suggest an afternoon on the sofa watching festive movies, they mutter things about wishing they were Home Alone.

And the idea of afternoons spent baking Rudolph biscuits gets cut off at Santa's pass when they point out that I can buy a yule log at the corner shop for a pound.

I've tried looking on the bright side. At least Spider and Darthie no longer spend all of December immersed in that little nugget of hope and optimism, otherwise known as the Argos catalogue. I no longer spend Christmas Eve building a Teenage Ninja fort that requires the brainpower of a nuclear physicist and the patience of Saint Donatello Michelangelo of the Blessed Leonardo Raphael.

We get more sleep. The living room doesn't look like the interior of a skip by 9 a.m. They now pitch in and help with dinner. And I don't have to spend twenty minutes persuading them that Brussels sprouts give them super powers.

But fellow members of Crimbo PANTS know it's just not the same, so this year, I'm relying on a different superhero to deliver the goods I'd like to wake up to at 5.30 a.m. on Christmas morning.

Dear Santa, give me a shout if you need a hand to wrap a time machine, a penguin protection order, Jenga and a video of Humph the Camel, circa 2005. ◆

2015

Mum Wages and Teenage Stages ››››

Paying Mum

What would you do if you suddenly came into £172K a year?

That's enough money to buy a seat on a space flight. Or get two packets of Revels at the cinema. Or colonise an uninhabited island and name it after someone you love. Hi, I'm Shari Low, Queen of the Isle of Liam Neeson.

According to a new study, £172K would be a mum's annual salary if all the vital aspects of her role were charged at standard rates.

Incidentally, memo to my teenage sons: I'll take it in cash or you can pay me in Curly Wurlies.

However, let's get real. If motherhood was an occupation, there would be standards and targets. Unless I was going to do a Nick Clegg (be entirely ineffectual but still pocket my wages), I think my brood might want a refund on services that are decidedly below par.

If living in Chez Low was reviewed on TripAdvisor, I'd get three stars and comments like 'landlady not at her best in mornings' and 'food is hit or miss'.

The salary calculation took into account roles including head chef, chauffeur, teacher, counsellor, cleaner and personal shopper.

My performance-related pay would immediately face PAYE deductions – Pay As You Eat. My culinary failings are legendary. I cook everything at 220 degrees and frequently forget what's in the oven, resulting in potato wedges that could be used as missiles should we ever need to defend our shores.

I do operate a four-times-a-day chauffeur service, but there would be penalties for late arrivals and damage to the company jalopy. This week two tyres – count them, TWO – have fallen victim to the national scourge of the pothole, and I lost a wing mirror to a car coming the other way on a narrow road.

In the teaching category, it's probably time the NEU (National Education Union) had me sacked. A few nights ago, I tried to help my junior Einstein with physics homework, despite the fact that I am to circuits and amps what Jeremy Clarkson is to diplomacy and peaceful resolution. I googled the answer, then pretended I came up with it myself. And – oh the shame – it was wrong. If you're looking for me, I'll be in the corner writing a 1,000 lines of 'I must not pretend I once worked for NASA'.

In our house, counselling is a see-saw that frequently tips in the wrong direction. I'm regularly stressed, a tad neurotic, a hypochondriac, and at the moment I'm on an unfeasibly tight deadline for the next novel – so hello, sleep deprivation.

Paying Mum

I'd love to say I handle potential issues in a calm, logical manner, but I prefer to go straight to panic and doom until someone talks me down from acute hysteria.

I've delegated most of the cleaning. If they're big enough to operate a Playstation, they're big enough to pilot the washing machine and the Hoover.

And, finally, my personal shopping skills have been firmly rejected. I'm no longer allowed to buy their clothes, and I fear they'll use the flashbacks to the polar bear onesies and childhood pictures of me dressing them in matching outfits as mitigating reasons not to visit me when I'm old.

So that £172K annual salary? After deductions, penalties, and payments for sub-contracting the cleaning duties, my calculations suggest that I'm running at a deficit.

Boys, I owe you a tenner.

Do you want it in cash or Curly Wurlies?

Love, Mum xx ◆

The Wonder Years

So it's finally happened. Sob. I woke up one day this week and realised that Clichés of Parenthood, number 132, is absolutely true. In case you're not privy to the Encyclopaedia of Mumdom, number 132 sits right after 'You will one day accuse them of treating the house like a hotel' and 'No, boys never learn to put the seat down'.

But back to the ominous 132: they do indeed grow up too fast.

Low the Elder is fourteen and, a few days ago, I became the mother of two teenagers when Low the Younger turned thirteen. How can that be? I still haven't lost my baby weight.

My eldest son now towers over me. He wears men's clothes. He has a deep voice. What happened to the little kid who refused to leave the house unless he was wearing his Buzz Lightyear pants? Incidentally, if you see a tall youth reading this page and suddenly crumbling in a pile of embarrassment, you'll know that's the boy formerly known as the Defender of the Universe.

The Wonder Years

So here we go, boldly into that black hole of teenage years. Apparently, I can look forward to hormonal surges, slamming doors, defiant behaviour, pushing boundaries, deliberate disobedience and cries of 'I'm not listening to you!'

Although, I'm not sure if that relates to their advancing years or my looming menopause.

However, fellow parents, I'm refusing to give in to the possibility of years of teenage challenges. In fact, I've made a decision – I'm going to get in first.

Yep, I'm throwing a rebellion.

For the last thirteen years, I've been a paragon of good behaviour. I don't drink, so no rolling in at 4 a.m. clutching a kebab and singing an Elvis medley.

Actually, I do roll in at 4 a.m. with a kebab and an Elvis medley but only on special occasions. Birthdays. Anniversaries. Tuesdays.

But the point is, for the last thirteen wonderful but hectic years, my life has been at their disposal. They come first. I don't remember the last time I went shopping for clothes and actually took a day to wander round the shops. Now, it's a quick online splurge between basketball, rugby and the school run.

So, my darling sons, be warned – from now on I'm reverting to teendom. I'm going to spend two hours getting ready to go out. I will also take 231 selfies at every stage of the preparations.

I'm going to snapchat my pals every five minutes. I may

have to learn how to do that first. Then teach aforementioned pals. We're dinosaurs. We still use the telephone for speaking.

I'm not going to tidy my room until it looks like it's been in the path of a tornado and requires breathing apparatus to enter.

I'm going to make plans. Big plans. Liam Neeson posters are going on my wall and I'll spend hours daydreaming about our future children. I'll ignore the obvious – that Liam's fantasy families tend to get kidnapped by evil gangs and then he has to issue threats in a low voice before wiping out a subcontinent in order to find them.

I'm going to experiment with new substances. I'm way too old and wise to start smoking or sniffing anything, so I was thinking I'd maybe try hummus. Or Quorn.

Oh, and I'm going to tell everyone in the house that they know nothing and I'm always right. Actually, I do that already.

So, my sons, I love you and I apologise in advance for what you're about to witness. You are, of course, welcome to inform me of any concerns. I assure you they'll be dealt with in an appropriate manner.

Try not to be offended when I tell you I'm not listening to you. ◆

Mumflu

Gents, I apologise for the crushing blow I'm about to deliver. It's long been acknowledged that Manflu is the worst of all ailments. I've listened to years of claims that nothing – not even childbirth – comes close to the suffering of a male with a temperature.

However, budge over blokes, because I've now discovered that you don't win the poorly prize.

I've just spent a week at the mercy of a virus that took me to the very brink of despair. Forget Manflu – I've had Mumflu.

It had all the symptoms of the general flu – raised temperature, sweats, chills, sore head, weak limbs, sneezes, and a cough that sounds like three corgis singing Tom Jones songs on the karaoke.

But Mumflu also comes with a crushing psychological blow – in the midst of my snot-fuelled anguish, I learned that I'm not, in fact, indispensable.

Sorry, had to stop and clutch my chest in a dramatic fashion after typing that last sentence.

How can that be? How can this house continue to function when I'm not there, in the trenches, co-ordinating Operation Low?

On a normal day, I'm the one hustling my teenage sons out to school, checking showers are taken, teeth are brushed, and attempting to limit hair-gelling to less than five minutes.

I organise their routines with military precision: homework, school run, lunches, after-school activities, chores and sport. They're both basketball players and train most nights, so there's another set of runs, kits and strategic planning for weekend games that take place all over the country.

Logistics aside, I counsel them when they have worries, shop for nutritious meals, make sure they eat at the right time, and remind them that a strawberry tart doesn't count as one of their five a day.

My parenting extends to our pooch, who gets walked, fed and reassured that she is in fact the most gorgeous labradoodle in the nation.

Wifely duties are also in the mix. Love, affection, laughs and trying not to mention the words 'mid-life crisis' when he comes home from the shops sporting a brand-new bomber jacket. Incidentally, honey, I love you, but I hope you kept the receipt.

Mumflu

Then there's general housework, cooking, cleaning, washing, ironing, refereeing, arranging our social lives, planning holidays and paying bills.

And, in between all that, I work full time.

In short, I'm the knackered lynchpin of the Lows, the person at the core of the family who gets through it all by telling herself that they couldn't do it without me, that their lives would come crashing down if I wasn't there to handle their sweaty kit bags in the manner of radioactive waste.

But no more. Sob. Saint Shari of the Control Freakery Motherhood came down with the flu and, for the first time ever, I was forced to take to my chambers for three days of shivers, sweats and self-pity.

And yet... the world kept turning. I expected to emerge blinking into the sunlight, to a family on the edge of meltdown. Apparently not.

They made it to school. They made it to training. I've no idea what they ate or drank, but they seem to still be functioning, so I'm guessing they didn't spend seventy-two hours eating nothing but Cheesy Wotsits. The house looks like it's been ransacked, the washing pile belongs in the Pyrenees, and I'm fairly sure they're wearing odd socks, but they're fine. Even the labradoodle seems nonplussed.

How can that be? Couldn't they even have pretended that it had all gone to hell without me? Oh, the pain. The suffering.

Gents, you have it easy – Manflu usually disappears after a few days of sympathy and pampering.

But Mumflu? Paracetamol and bed might sort out the virus, but realising that you're not needed leaves scars that will last a lifetime. Sniff. ◆

School of Life

Sometimes the obvious is just staring you in the slightly terrifying face. Partick Thistle's new mascot, Kingsley, was unveiled this week, and the general reaction has been on the evil clown side of horror. Some claim it resembles a Dementor from Harry Potter. Some say it's more like the love child of Lisa Simpson and a Chuckie doll.

I beg to differ. I feel poor Kingsley is misunderstood and see a whole other range of emotions. I see worry, I see fear, I see panic. When you add in the auspicious timing, it becomes obvious that Kingsley's expression is inspired by a woefully familiar sight at this time of year.

He's a parent at the start of the summer holidays.

Six weeks. Six long weeks of entertaining the kids, organising child supervision and spending the equivalent of a fortnight in the Bahamas on a day trip to the cinema.

I'm lucky to work from home. It gives flexibility, even if I'm usually still at my laptop at 4 a.m. However, in the summer holidays, managing the work/life ratio requires the kind of juggling expertise usually demonstrated by large-footed, red-nosed chaps called Coco and Krusty.

In the primary school years, I'd make grand plans to keep my boys busy. I'd organise bike rides, footie in the garden, painting and cosy afternoons reading and doing craft-like stuff I remember from *Blue Peter* circa 1977.

Invariably, rubbish weather, an imminent book deadline and a baking-obsessed son would result in days spent typing a romcom with one hand, while tent-building, watching Pixar DVDs, and supervising the creation of so many cupcakes I'd have to thrust strawberry-sprinkled fairy sponges into the hands of innocent passersby.

Now, and I can't believe I'm saying this, I've realised that I miss the old days.

My boys have grown into teens who are usually too busy to lie in bed until teatime. So far, so good. On the downside, I now appear to be in a *Twilight Zone* episode called Mum'll Take Me.

We live in an area that has little public transport, so their summer days consist of the following:

Wake up, go to gym to work out.

How are you getting there? Mum'll take me.

Arrange to meet pals to play basketball in the afternoon.

How are you getting there? Mum'll take me.

Over to a friend's house for dinner?

No problem, Mum'll take me.

More basketball training in the evening?

Mum'll take me.

Then, just for a little bit of variety…

Friends coming here afterwards, then need to get home?

Mum'll take them.

Every now and then, I get clingy and throw in a curve ball. 'I'll come to the gym with you today, son. You know, so we can spend time together.'

At which point son faints. Quick visit to pharmacist for smelling salts?

Mum'll take him.

This summer, in a typical masterstroke of inferior time management, I'm chasing a book deadline yet again, so I'll spend most of my days sitting in car parks outside sport centres, gyms and eating establishments, banging out another chapter of romantic comedy while waiting for my sons to reappear.

Their schedule? Fun, fitness, friends. Mine? Drive. Work. Drive. Work. Drive. Work.

So, parents of primary kids, enjoy it while you can. Savour the footie in the garden. Enjoy the tent-building. And all those cupcakes? If you see a burd sitting in a car park typing a novel on her laptop, she'd really appreciate the ones with the strawberry sprinkles. ◆

Fleeing the Nest

I've heard about the potential pitfalls of empty nest syndrome.

Optimist that I am, though, I reckoned I had it sussed. When my boys leave home and my fingers are finally prised off their ankles, I had planned to simply shrug off my cloak of control-freak motherdom and get on with doing all the things that I never seem to have time for.

I'd fill my days doing yoga, cooking healthy meals from scratch and catching up on highbrow discussion programmes that expand the intellect.

Please note, I realise that last paragraph comes with a measure of delusion, given that I tried yoga once and pulled a muscle, I am to cooking what Jamie Oliver is to chicken nuggets, and my idea of highbrow telly is a *Criminal Minds* box set.

But life would go on. I might even turn into one of those suave, chic types who has time to slap on make-up every morning and check she's not wearing her leggings backwards. Apologies to all those who witnessed my unfortunate gait on the school run last Wednesday.

However, I've just had a taste of a child-free existence and I now know that the future is not how I imagined. Apparently, the minute the kids are gone, I'll regress to being Shari Low, age eighteen and three-quarters.

I've said before that both the Low teenagers are sporty types. However, not wishing to come across as Show-Off Shaz, I didn't mention that they both play basketball for Scotland in their respective age groups.

Yes, check out my chunky ways and embrace the irony that I bred two national athletes – a genetic miracle, since I'm definitely more Murray Mint than Judy Murray. Although, I was wing-attack in our school's unbeaten netball team of 1983.

Anyway, last weekend, Low the Elder was playing for Scotland against Ireland in Dublin.

Off I went, with another very lovely basketball mum (henceforth known as VLBM) to support the team. Now, what you have to understand is that both myself and VLBM are organisational supremos, who facilitate every requirement of our broods' packed itineraries. We plan. We research. We implement. And we get everyone where they're meant to be, when they need to be there, with everything they need to have.

We run ships that are tighter than my Spanx after a

weekend on the banoffee pies – until, it would seem, the point when we're only accountable for our own schedules.

We stepped off the plane at Dublin airport, expecting to be met with prearranged transport, only to realise that I'd forgotten to arrange it. We headed to the hotel, ready to turn in at a sensible hour, only to be waylaid at the bar.

We then sat up gabbing until 3.30 a.m. Note to the G8 Leaders, we sorted out the entire world. I'll send you a memo with our notes.

Next morning I woke at 9 a.m., jumped out of bed, did four hours' work, went for a ten-mile jog, before a kale salad lunch.

Okay, I'm lying. I did wake at 9 a.m., but lazed until noon. Mumflu aside, I haven't stayed in bed until midday since 1986. Our only workout was a walk to a restaurant, and we ate puddings for lunch.

Other than attending the games, where we cheered our boys in a raucous manner, the rest of the weekend had no organisation whatsoever. Just sheer indulgence, laughs and the complete abdication of responsibility.

Empty nest syndrome? Bring it on. Boys, I'll miss you. But when one teenager leaves, apparently another one takes its place.

Signed,

Shari Low,

Age eighteen and three-quarters. ◆

All About Me

Och, you've got to love that modest wee lamb, Heather Mills. The ex-wife of Paul McCartney has been wittering forth on the extent of their parental influences in bringing up their daughter Beatrice.

Heather said, 'I think she's got the best of both of us. We're both very musical, I taught her the saxophone because her father can't read music so I do all the music teaching.'

Ah, the passive-aggressive triumph of claiming glory while pointing out another's failings. Cue theme tune for musical Heather's very own version of an Andrew Lloyd Webber classic – Catty.

In a further barb to her ex, Heather went on to say that Beatrice believes 'she is ninety-nine per cent me'.

I'm not judging, but personally speaking, achieving that kind of parent/child similarity isn't on my list of family aspirations.

Dear sons, if you ever read this, let me say right here and

now, that I sincerely hope you never become ninety-nine per cent me. I have a gazillion flaws and they're all mine, so please get your own.

There's no doubt that my boys have inherited a couple of my characteristics. Fourteen-year-old Low the Elder is a dedicated athlete who loves a party, a laugh, and rarely comes through the front door without five pals in tow. His priority list is sport, pals, food. Swap sport for 'impulsive online shopping' and his shiny new parachute (eBay £99.99) would drop him on my side of the personality fence.

At thirteen, son number two is a dedicated bookworm – a big tick in the 'got this from his mother' box. Other than that, he's laid-back, chilled out and naturally happy in his own skin – all traits that are in direct contrast to the fact that I'm more highly strung than Billy Connolly's banjo. If musical talent is genetic, Low the Younger's skills on the saxophone would suggest I had a one-night stand with Kenny G. And I can assure you I'm not responsible for his vocal talent, given that I couldn't hold a tune in Noel Gallagher's Tupperware box.

I recently read the wise words of a retiring headmaster, who claimed that too many parents were damaging their children's development with their narcissistic endeavours to turn their children into mini-me's.

In our house, that's already a physical impossibility, given that my offspring are six feet tall. But anatomical anomalies aside, the list of attributes I hope my children do not inherit is long.

All About Me

Obviously I'd prefer them to avoid two of my most prevalent features: my rubbish metabolism and my fondness for a pudding.

I pray they don't develop my capacity for relentless worry. Right now, I'm worrying they'll get my worry gene. And don't get me started on my catastrophising, otherwise my blood pressure might increase, I could faint, fall to the ground, setting off an earth tremor that could wipe out the Western world.

Which brings me to my chronic hypochondria. I'd tell you more about it but I'm too busy googling the symptoms and treatment for 'high blood pressure and fainting'.

I'm impatient. Intolerant. Shallow. When riled, my choice of language makes Gordon Ramsay look like Mary Berry. On a Sunday. At church.

And decades of juggling house, work and family have left me way too far along the scale of dogmatic control freakery. Why? Because I said so.

So creating mini-me's? No thanks. Boys, my advice is to be unique, be different, be yourself. However, if you do experience moments of worry, hypochondria, or second helpings of pudding, there are flippers on eBay that are perfect for the very occasional splash in your mother's gene pool. ◆

Term Time Blues

Many things in life are predictable. Death. Taxes. Donald Trump conserving his hairdo by avoiding high-wind situations.

And the wails of devastation that ring out in Casa Low at this time every year. No, it's not because we've once again managed to go a whole summer without unpacking the swanky double sun lounger – codename Optimism Central – that the husband still hasn't forgiven me for buying.

It's because it's that time again; the dark day I hate even more than the January morning on which I put away the singing penguins and say goodbye to two weeks of festive revelry.

My boys go back to school today.

No more stress-free, chilled-out mornings. No more laughs and blethers throughout the day. No more cups of tea, brought to me with love and demands for a minimum wage.

Sorry, had to pause for a solemn moment of self-pity.

I know it's pathetic. I realise some of my pals are putting out the bunting and waving their wee darlings off to the accompanying soundtrack of a brass band, but I'm sadder than Miley Cyrus in a polo neck jumper.

The uniforms are ironed and the brand-new PE kit is packed – the same one I'll soon be picking up after a double sports session and transporting to the washing machine in the same manner I'd treat plutonium.

But logistical preparations aside, I'm just not ready to start the new term, and once again become Ascending Mum. For the uninformed, that's the maternal equivalent of the phone ringtone that gets louder the longer you ignore it.

This is followed by the daily uniform hunt, because even if I've left their tie in a visible place, attached to flashing lights and a claxon that sounds at ten-minute intervals, it's always gone in the morning.

Then there are the standard morning calls of the species, teenagerous boyus.

'I can't find my PE kit!'

'I forgot to do my homework.'

And my personal favourite, 'We were supposed to take something in today. Oh yes. A rocket for our science project,' he says, as we're stepping into the car.

He then wonders why I'm banging my head off the outside of the window.

Next, comes the biggest bugbear of all: the school run numpties. Oh, how I've missed them for the last six weeks.

Not. There are the ones who just stop in the middle of the road to let their little angels out. Or equally infuriating, park on a corner, forcing all the other vehicles to adopt a one-way system to get past them.

As I fight to refrain from pointing out the error of their ways, inside my jalopy, Ascending Mum is back.

'Have you got everything you need for today?'

'Yes, Mum,' one of them answers.

'Are you positive you've got everything?'

'Yes, Mum.'

'You've DEFINITELY got everything?'

Sigh. Eye roll. 'Yes!'

And off they boldly go, oozing confidence and independence, which lasts until two minutes after I get back in the house and the phone call comes, the one that starts, 'Mum, I forgot to bring...'

So, I'm sad. Devastated. The only consolation is that the education they'll receive can be used for my benefit.

Boys, any chance of doing Ascending Mum a favour and using your mathematical expertise to work out how many days until the mid-term break? ◆

Spectre

You'd have to be living under Daniel Craig's shed to avoid the hype surrounding the release of the new Bond movie, *Spectre*.

Next weekend, I'll be handing over my tenner at the multiplex, remortgaging the house to fund a large Coke and a cardboard tray of nachos, and then trying to sit through two hours without snapping at the people behind me for rustling their popcorn while Bond, James Bond's finely toned abs are saving the world.

There's been much speculation over who will take over from Craig, Daniel Craig if he hangs up his deadly blue swimmies.

I have a suggestion. If they're looking for someone who already has the required skill set, the next Earth-saving super spy should be… an undercover mum.

It makes absolute sense to harness the powers of maternal experience.

First of all, we can spot guilt at a hundred paces. Oh yes, my darling Low juniors, we can. Even when neither of you were 'fessing up to the great 'Toilet Duck puddle on the new carpet' debacle of 2006, I knew exactly which one of you was guilty. One day, retribution will be mine, so when you move into your own flat, you might want to put a lock on the cupboard under the sink if I'm round for a visit.

Which brings me neatly to the next point: we forget nothing. Every comment, every crime, every misspoken word is stored, ready to be trotted out like a court transcript when required for historical accuracy, emotional blackmail or bargaining power.

We would be naturals at undercover work and talking our way out of tight spots due to our awe-inspiring competence in falsehoods and duplicity. I give you the Tooth Fairy, the Easter Bunny, and the chunky bloke in the red suit.

Our interrogation skills are on a level that is comparable with the CIA and we also know when to tap into our extensive network of intelligence sources. 'Where were you? What were you doing? Who were you with? AND DON'T DARE LIE OR I'LL CHECK WITH THEIR MOTHER!'

We're also relentlessly proficient at sensing danger and monitoring potentially hazardous situations. That's why we immediately go straight to hyper-alert at crucial milestones: the first day at school, participation in sporting events, and later, solo outings and teenage parties. Don't get me started on the first holiday with the pals. My sons will be followed and subjected to 24-hour covert surveillance should they ever decide to embark on a fortnight in Magaluf with their chums.

Of course, there are downsides to a career in espionage. Lady spies look great in Diana Rigg leather trousers. Given that my diet has failed spectacularly this year, encasing my lower half in leather would make me look suspiciously like a two-seater sofa.

Then there's the ever-present threat of being annihilated by a lethal psychopath with a secret island lair. Or having to stroll out of the local beach looking alluring in form-fitting blue swimmies. I'm not sure the population of Millport is up for the spectacle.

But let's face it, it's a far more appealing prospect than being a Bond girl. All that waiting around for him to conquer evil would undoubtedly drive me to boredom-snack on my trusty Tunnock's teacakes, and then James would have to add 'helping me wrestle out of my Spanx' to his list of heroic feats.

So producers of the Bond franchise, when you're looking for the next 'double Oh-Dear-God is that thing loaded?' I'm here, I'm ready and I'll expect your call.

The name? Low. Shari Low. ✦

Woe Ho Ho

I'm making an official Christmas crime complaint.

Officer, someone stole the first half of December.

It seems like only yesterday that it was November and I had plans. A schedule. A strategy.

I was going to be supremely organised for the festivities, one of those irritants with flashing snowman earrings who opens her advent calendar every day and takes out another little parcel of smugness.

Oh yes, I was aiming for full-scale premature elfjaculation.

Then I woke up and it was just over a week until Christmas and I'm as prepared as Rudolph begging for a nasal decongestant at the late-night chemist on the 24th of December.

Worse, I'm in this sorry state despite studying one of those magazine guides that promises to turn a failed yuletide domestic goddess into a cross between Mary Berry, Nigella Lawson, Kirstie Allsopp and the ferocious one out of Kim & Aggie.

It looked so easy.

Week one – put up the decorations, and send handwritten cards, taking care to include a personal, heartfelt yet catchy line of affectionate greeting.

Week two – wrap carefully chosen presents in paper that matches the colour scheme of the beautifully adorned tree.

Week three – whip the house into spectacular shape, cleaning all the places that are ignored for most of the year. Yes, you, skirting boards. Be afraid, cupboard under the sink.

Then, while humming along to the Michael Bublé Christmas album, place orders for the ingredients required to prepare a culinary masterpiece.

In between all that, I intended to uphold my very own annual Christmas tradition. This consists of acknowledging that, once again, I haven't lost the five stones required to get into a sexy Mrs Claus outfit, and thus calling on the entire family to give me a punty into the loft for my trusty old Santa suit. No padding required. Sob.

Sadly, I've achieved none of the above.

I fully expect to be sacked from the Parents' Advent, Nativity, Tinsel & Santa League. Or Crimbo PANTS League for short.

In my defence, I have a big ole sack of excuses. I got caught up on a work project that required endless late-night hours at the keyboard.

Husband has done nothing because he's under the impression that a Christmas fairy arrives every year, waves a wand and everything from the cranberry sauce to the mandatory Jenga magically appears.

Low the Elder, our devoted basketball player, broke a bone in his foot, necessitating countless trips to physios, orthopaedic consultants, sports injury clinics and specialist podiatrists. Please note that I embarked on this intensive regime of consultation and treatment despite the fact that I'm fairly sure I qualify as a medical expert after watching every episode of *ER* and being the family champion at Operation fourteen years in a row.

Meanwhile, Low the Younger and his saxophone were practising for his school show. It's difficult to concentrate on choosing the perfect yule log when there's a perpetual background soundtrack of 'The Twelve Days of Christmas'. On the first day of Christmas, my true love gave to me – tinnitus.

I've got one week to pull it back, get back on the tinsel track while accepting that the Low clan's nativity scene will look very different to the conventional one.

The father and his roasting chestnuts will be oblivious in front of the telly, the three wise men will be pondering a shepherd's cracked metatarsal bone, and the bright star will still be playing 'The Twelve Days of Christmas' on the saxophone.

And the mother of the family?

Just follow the sounds of the Michael Bublé Christmas album to the red-trousered legs sticking out from the cupboard under the sink.

Woe, ho, ho. ◆

The Hypocritical Oath

Can I open by requesting that if anyone spots one of my teenage sons reading this, please remove it from him immediately? If he's already yelling a furious, 'I knew it!' it's too late.

Hopefully, it'll be years from now, when I'm in the Home for Decrepit Old Bonkbuster Authors, before my offspring will look back through my columns, spot this page, and realise my motherhood philosophies were a sham.

You see, my name is Shari Low and I'm a founding member of The Association of Parental Hypocrites. My family life is an outrageous collusion of subterfuge and double standards.

Food: I've always preached that my children follow the 'five portions of fruit and veg a day' rule. I do the same. Although mine are an apple Danish, a banoffee pie, strawberry jam, and a Hawaiian pizza, which counts as two because there's pineapple and a tomato-based sauce.

Housekeeping: Rooms must be kept tidy. Except my

boudoir, which frequently looks like someone's shot the entire stock of New Look's plus-size department out of a canon and it's landed on my floor.

Fitness: Since they were small, I've instilled the benefits of exercise. I, on the other chubby hand, consider a bicep curl to be the motion of getting a choccie digestive from the packet to my gob.

Sleep: Eight hours a night is essential – attests the insomniac author who can regularly be found thumping the keyboard at 5 a.m.

Worry: 'There's no point in fretting,' I witter, coming over all Doris Day and crooning 'Que Sera Sera', before heading to a dark corner to sweat over my 234th irrational fear of the day.

Education: 'School years are crucial and what you learn will serve you well in life,' I preach. The truth? I've never had to deploy Pythagoras' theorem or make the stewed apples we learned to concoct in first-year Home Economics.

Finances: Boys, spend wisely! My bank manager is now holding his sides, laughing hysterically.

Social media: I limit their online activity, condemning this modern phenomenon as trite, while doing a Facebook quiz that informs me my elf name is Cookie the Tinsel Toed Fruit Cake.

Vices: No. Smoking. Ever – demands the woman who spent high school lunchtimes round the back of the sheds with my two nicotine chums, Benson & Hedges.

Relationships: I warn them that they should never, ever enter a relationship with someone who's clingy... while praying they'll never leave me.

I also advise them to delay serious romance until they're older. Meanwhile, at their age, I was already planning a glorious future with the second love of my life. Please note, this was only because the first love of my life, Martin Kemp from Spandau Ballet, hadn't swept me off to a life of rock star excess. Yes, I knew that much was true.

Ambition: Have a plan. Know what you want in life but be realistic. Incidentally, I'm still fairly sure Mr Kemp will turn up any minute.

This week, my shameful hypocrisy has been brought into sharp focus by Low the Elder's prelims. My droning insistence that he studies is somewhat ironic, considering that the only time I ever opened a revision book was to cover up the fact that I was reading Jackie Collins's *Hollywood Wives* behind it.

So son, if you read this one day, I apologise for the manipulation and I'm sorry if all this work hasn't paid off.

But if it has?

Please know that you don't have to thank me. No, really. Your love and happiness are reward enough.

And perhaps the delivery of a banoffee pie to the Home for Decrepit Old Bonkbuster Authors. It's one of my five a day. ◆

2016

School Exams and Celebrity Prams »»»

The Parent Label

I'm not a fan of labels. Unless, that is, they're on gorgeous handbags and come with the tantalising promise of a bargain-tastic eighty per cent off in the sale.

Once upon a time, I had the shoulder pads and mullet of a YUPPIE, but, sadly, not the bank balance. Husband and I were DINKYs for a while (Double Income, No Kids Yet), but then our little darlings came along and made us KNACKERED. Please note, that last one isn't an acronym.

My general aversion to group terms was exacerbated this week, when I experienced an identity crisis after reading research on parenting labels, some of which I didn't even know existed.

I am, of course, familiar with the concept of the Tiger Mother: controlling dictators who enforce a strict regime that demands success. We've all met them. Their children speak six languages and can play Liszt's 'Hungarian Rhapsody No. 2' on the piano while reciting trigonometry equations and memorising the fundamentals of nuclear physics. At age six.

Then there's the Helicopter Parent. Nope, not Prince Andrew. It's the uptight, ultra-vigilant control freak that hovers at the edge of the ball crawl, giving stares of warning to any child that comes within three feet of their little prodigy. Similarly, the Drone Parent also indulges in relentless surveillance, but does it in a silent manner.

It's easy to be confused by the traits of the Snowplough Parent. It doesn't mean someone who is funded by the council, difficult to manoeuver and only comes out in inclement weather. It actually refers to manipulative elders who remove any obstacle from their offspring's path, thereby ensuring they always get where they want to go.

On the other end of the overbearing scale is the Free-Range Parent, who encourages their kid to explore the world, thereby fostering independence and confidence. Fair enough. But if a seven-year-old gets on the Megabus clutching a suitcase and two weeks' pocket money, it's only reasonable to expect a free-range call from social services.

The Submarine Parent keeps a low profile, only surfacing in times of trouble. I wouldn't mind being one of those, if, like the latest MoD deal, it came with a government investment of £205 billion.

Jellyfish Parents can cause prolonged irritation. These are the pushovers that refuse to discipline their precious angel, and believe that if Princess Rainbow Trixielullah is running around a restaurant squealing at a decibel level that cracks the glass on prawn cocktail bowls, it's perfectly fine because it means she is 'expressing herself'.

At first glance, I wondered if I was a member of the Lighthouse Parenting gang, thanks to my unfortunate, accidental flashing of the holy Spanx in windy situations. But no. The intended meaning of this terminology is far more poetic. The lighthouse mother is a guiding 'beacon of light', allowing her youths to safely navigate the world and ride the waves of life. It's close, but not quite applicable to me. The last time my sons rode the waves of life it involved a pedalo, cost ten euros for half an hour and I pulled a hamstring.

So, after much consideration, I've realised that I don't conform to any of the existing labels, and decided to invent one of my own.

Ladies and gentlemen, my name is Shari and I'm a Wellie Boot Mum. I like to think I'm warm, reliable and protect my brood from the worst of life's storms.

I'm also a bit old-fashioned, slightly cumbersome, occasionally embarrassing and out of place in posh company.

But, hey, I can always be dressed up with a gorgeous handbag that was a bargaintastic eighty per cent off in a sale. ◆

Testing Times

Welcome to the Easter school holidays. Or as they're known in this house, The National Fortnight of No, You Can't Have a Yorkie Egg For Breakfast.

Incidentally, I've no idea why the school break didn't actually encompass the annual celebration this year. I've a hunch that the reason our little darlings had to pop back to school for a few days between the holiday weekend and their fortnight off, was due to some kind of marketing collaboration with Scottish Slimmers. I'm admitting nothing, but the evidence does show that, in that period, three of my broods' eggs mysteriously disappeared, while I gained two pounds.

However, overlooking the bite-sized glitches of scheduling, egg theft and breakfast dietary debates, the Easter holibags have always been my favourite time of the year.

Please note, this excludes the dark events of April 2007, when, desperate to prove to the five- and seven-year-old Junior Lows that I was cool, I careered down our driveway on Low the Younger's skateboard. Sadly, the equipment wasn't meant for a woman of the same approximate weight as Kate Moss sitting in a Ford Focus eating a Lindt bunny. I was verging on impressive, when two wheels suddenly snapped off, shot through the glass panel of the front door, and I spent a fortnight in Stookie Central.

That painful flashback aside, the spring break generally brings bring two weeks of release from the school run, without the stresses of Christmas or running up the overdraft on a fortnight in Torremolinos.

It's a blissful interlude of relaxation during which everything is made better by a stockpile of Rolos.

Until now.

HNC in Parenthood, Module 2,945: The Ambush of Educational Milestones.

Why, oh why, did no-one warn me about the stresses that suddenly descend when your child is facing important exams?

Low the Elder sits his National 5s in May. In the old days, when mullets ruled and I was going to marry the bloke from Spandau Ballet, they were called O Grades.

I vaguely remember them. Studying involved reading *Jackie* magazine (English), having tea with my granny (history), working out if I had enough money for a packet of Benson & Hedges (maths), exploring my boyfriend's tonsils (biology) and embracing the entire back catalogue of Heaven 17 (music).

But that was then.

Somehow, now that I'm an MP (Meddling Parent), I've become that person that I thought I'd never be: that mother who prints out schedules, researches study methods, and frets over timescales.

All this strain has caused a sudden, yet seismic shift (geography: earthquakes, tectonic plates, natural disasters) in my mothering style.

Gone is the 'laid-back, let's do something fun, woo-hoo it's the holidays' mum, and in her place is a highly-strung imposter who comes out with phrases like, 'If you fail to prepare, you prepare to fail.'

'Do as I say, not as I did.'

And – my toes are curling with shame – 'You'll thank me for this one day.'

The irony is that Low the Elder is taking it all in his stride, but I'm having sleepless nights, panicking about the laws of precipitation and 1,000-word discursive essays. Oh, and when I get to the Pearly Gates, Mr Pythagoras had better do a runner before he gets a boot in the hypotenuse.

Son, if you're reading this, I just want you to know that all that matters is that you do your best. And look on the bright side – you only have to do this once. Meanwhile, I've just revised the statistics section of my HNC in Parenthood, and it's only 732 days until I get to do this all again with your brother.

Pass the Rolos. ◆

Baby Payne

Ladies, hang on to your breast pumps, because an extraordinary event is gripping the headlines. Forget the US presidential race. Don't worry about Brexit or the crashing pound. Ignore all those pesky wars. According to social media coverage, what really matters is that a celebrity with a chequered love history and a bloke that used to be a fully gelled-up boy band member may or may not be expecting the pitter patter of tiny Prada bootees.

Sigh.

I caught sight of a full-scale keyboard battle on the comments section of a celebrity website the other day (please don't judge me – my copy of *War and Peace* was in the wash), with two trolls furiously debating whether or not Cheryl Tweedy Cole Fernandez Versini Maybe Soon Payne should confirm or deny her maternal imminence.

Is this what we've come to? People who don't even know each other are having fierce, profane, online arguments about another woman's prenatal decisions. Neanderthal man, if you're reading this, feel free to sue about that whole evolution thing.

The tattooed-bottom line is it's Cheryl's body. That makes it her choice on when to announce the pregnancy and put an end to the speculation.

In the meantime, one of the gossip mags (again, please don't judge – my Tolstoy collection was in the wash too) carried several pages of claims made by 'insiders', saying that Chezza has gone full Mumzilla. That's like Bridezilla, but with a steriliser unit and a subscription to *Mother & Baby* magazine.

According to the undoubtedly fabricated nonsense, her plans apparently include a £100K nursery flown in from LA, round-the-clock nannies, moving her mother in to help, babyproofing the house, and implementing an organic lifestyle.

Cheryl, I once sang along to a chorus of 'Something Kinda Oooh', so therefore I feel I know you well enough to give you my opinion.

If you are indeed cocooning a growing human under that designer coat, my advice would be to relax about the grand schemes and strategies.

When I was pregnant with son number one, I declared that the baby would eat only organic foods. I resolved to follow one of those baby eating and sleeping regimes that require the same logistical organisation as a space mission.

I vowed to read the classics aloud and play Mozart, thus guaranteeing my child would be a highbrow genius.

I painted clouds in the nursery. I considered buying a jogging pram so I could run round the park with my mini-Bolt. For the purposes of that deluded fantasy, I ignored the fact that I'd managed to successfully avoid galloping in public for the previous thirty-two years, so there was little chance it would be an event to be enjoyed while suffering sleep deprivation and cracked nipples.

Oh, and I absolutely, definitely swore there would be no dummy, no pre-packed baby food and no gimmicky clothing.

In reality? Fast forward a year and I'd broken just about every resolution in spectacular style. I'd swapped Mozart for Motown, the classics for the latest scandalous bonkbuster, jarred food was in the cupboard, we'd scrapped the overly strict schedule in favour of just being grateful when he slept, my trainers were still in the cupboard and my boy was dressed as a Christmas elf.

So Ms Tweedy Cole Fernandez Versini Maybe Soon Payne, if you are indeed expecting a new arrival, please don't make my mistake and fret over rules or plans. It's reproduction. It's part of life. And Neanderthal woman managed it without the experts, the nannies, or the hundred-grand nursery from LA. ◆

Gangsta Wrapper

Dear Mrs Claus,

I know you're not an agony aunt and problem resolution isn't your thing, but I thought I'd write to you because you must be sick of your husband getting all the mail at this time of year.

You see, I have a festive family tale of woe. The season of merriment has caused a generational identity crisis at Chez Low and our family is caught in the grip of a role reversal that is, quite frankly, ripping my tinsel.

It all started on Friday night. I was heading to a Christmas basketball tournament with my teenagers, and I donned a new T-shirt I'd bought for the occasion. As soon as they spotted my outfit, my two six-foot-two-inch strapping boys eyed me with pure fear.

'How do we stop her?' one said to the other, his voice tight with horror.

'Barricade the doors,' came the reply.

Gangsta Wrapper

Meanwhile, I looked down at my sparkly top, adorned with a huge Christmas present and the words, 'GANGSTA WRAPPER' and didn't see the problem at all.

Did I complain when six-year-old Low the Elder insisted on going everywhere dressed as an elf? No.

Did I object to the penguin onesie era of 2013? I don't believe I did.

Nor did I bat an eyelid when we were joined at the yuletide dinner table of 2008 by SpongeBob SquarePants and a camel.

Yet one slightly dodgy festive top and they're lining up a gift-wrapped barge pole with which to keep me at a distance, while muttering those three little words. 'You're. A. Beamer.'

Mrs C, if you're unfamiliar in the colloquial lingo, it means mortifying. Embarrassing. A scarlet-faced ruddy. Although, according to my brood, if you look it up in the dictionary you'll see a picture of me, wearing flashing snowman earrings, a Santa suit and reindeer socks.

Other points of peevedom? Before the big day, I'm now the one shaking the parcels under the tree while they look on with pitying tolerance.

On the 25th, I'll be up at the first smattering of reindeer dust, bursting to get proceedings underway, while they hide their heads under the duvet, hoping I'll fall back asleep so they can lie in until lunchtime.

I used to ration their sweets and worry about them getting a sugar rush. Now that they're athletes who don't eat junk, they give me the raised eyebrow of warning when I break open another box of Quality Street and threaten to prise it from my steely grasp.

They eat their Brussels sprouts without a murmur of complaint, and the pile left on my plate evokes comments like, 'Eat up your vegetables, Mum, they're good for you.'

As soon as lunch is cleared away, it's me who is dragging out the board games and begging them for a double bout of Monopoly and Pictionary. And, since I've invariably lost my specs, I now have to ask them for help in reading the words on the cards.

And they're the ones praying that I'll get so overtired that I'll conk out for a wee afternoon nap and leave them in peace to flop out on the couch and watch a movie.

Still, Mrs Claus, every Crimbo cloud. If you can't help with my issues, then at least be assured that we are happy to assist your family in the event of technical difficulties this year. If Rudolph is out of Night Nurse and too under the weather to head up the sleigh, I can offer my offspring. I'll pull the Gangsta Wrapper T-shirt back on and their beaming wee faces can lead the way.

Love, Shari ◆

2017

Worries, Woes, and Letting Go »»»

The Year of
No Worries

The toll of the bells signalling the dawn of 2017 had barely faded when I made my first resolution of the New Year.

12.05 a.m.: I, Shari Low, am going to stop worrying.

The husband noted the time and reminded me of it at 2 a.m., when I'd called Low the Elder Teenager for the second time to check he was enjoying the party he'd headed off to shortly after midnight.

Incidentally, for the uninitiated, 'check he was enjoying' is tense, overreactive, mother-speak for 'just making sure I don't need to call in a SWAT team because you're lost, have been kidnapped by aliens, or sucked into a sinister cult'.

It comes from the same dictionary of Maternal Double Talk as 'no, of course I would never spy on your texts or calls' (because 3,476 attempts to crack your phone password failed), and 'I'll always respect your privacy' (as long as you tell me everything I need to know, otherwise I'm entitled to call in professional interrogators and have you followed by a drone).

It's a given that, as the parent of two teens, a certain amount of low-level apprehension and fear of dark deeds comes with the job. Will they always be safe and happy? Will they achieve their dreams? And will they visit me in the home for Over-Anxious Maternal Doom Merchants when I'm old?

However, standard parental jitters aside, my aptitude for fretting is out of control. Over the years, I've made many vows to halt the handwringing, only to fail at the first hint of danger or woe.

A minor cough is a symptom of some rare, incurable, tropical affliction. I spent half of Boxing Day watching my family for signs of a toxic reaction to the dangerous combination of my cooking ineptitude and a pound of chipolatas.

And every time Trump churns out another irrational tweet, I remember that he will soon have access to the nuclear codes, whereby I hear the theme tune from the movie *Armageddon* and have a compelling urge to check out underground survival shelters on eBay.

It can't go on, because I'm now worried that my worrying worry will have worrying consequences for my health, after a needless panic resulted in actual physical damage. On a trip to Sofia last summer, I was walking along a street alone in the early evening, when I saw a chap coming towards me, exerting a general air of dodginess. I was so busy adopting a state of high alert, that I tripped over a kerb, and did a horizontal slide along the street like a tobogganist on black ice. I ended the display with a ceremonious faceplank, causing torn clothes, skint extremities, and a skeletal system that felt like it had been rearranged by a tumble dryer.

And the Scary Spectre of Dodginess? He helped me up, gathered my scattered belongings, and supported me as I hobbled into my hotel reception bearing a blood-soaked resemblance to an extra from the A&E department in *Grey's Anatomy*.

It has to stop. I want to be serene. Calm. A confident optimist.

So while I'm very aware that my hardcore catastrophising habit can't be undone in a flash (checks weather for risks of lightning or floods), my resolution for 2017 is to separate real issues from imaginary ones, keep things in perspective, and only be concerned about things that pose a clear and present danger.

After all, Low the Elder got back safely from his party. My cough is gone. No-one got food poisoning. And if you have any reassuring words about Trump, you'll find me in my shiny new bunker. ◆

Parent Fail

It's awards season, so please step forward TV presenter, Helen Skelton, and collect your Gong for Services to Parental Moments of Mortification.

Helen revealed on Twitter this week that she and her nineteen-month-old son Ernie had been banished from a playgroup.

She wrote, 'Worst day of my parenting life. Asked to leave after twenty mins. Screamed the place down…'

Helen, I share your pain, and can offer both good news and bad. The good news is that, on the grand scale of parenting episodes, this blip can be filed under 'Things You'll Laugh About When He's Twenty-One'.

The bad news? Take a deep breath. Now exhale. Don't be alarmed, but there will be many more 'worst days' to come.

When it comes to embarrassing moments, mistakes and mishaps, I think I'm probably into treble figures.

I once had to comfort-eat a box of Jaffa Cakes after my

two-year-old wedged himself into a shoe display in a busy shop and yelled the place down when I attempted to dislodge him.

Then there was the day in M&S, when I was squatting down to peruse the bottom-shelf bras, and one of my bored wee guys did a runner towards me, leapt on my back and sent me sprawling, taking an entire section of push up balconettes with me.

Holidays were a minefield of maternal catastrophes. On a trip to Cyprus, I delivered a stern health and safety warning. 'Do not, I repeat, DO NOT, run along the side of the pool. Promise?'

Six-year-old See-Me Bolt nodded obediently, then sprinted off, slipped and screeched all the way to Paphos A&E.

Other health and safety fails included my demonstration on how to properly use a fruit slicer, which all went a bit blood orange when I sheared the tip of my finger off. This was almost as smart as the day I attempted to teach them to safely use superglue and spent the next three hours trying to prise apart my thumbs.

And don't even get me started on the profanities. Twenty-two junior Ronaldos were given a lesson in vocabulary when my seven-year-old super-striker missed a penalty kick and shouted, 'Och for f***s sake'. When questioned, he explained, 'But that's what all Daddy's team say when they miss a goal.'

Husband was swiftly relegated to the subs bench.

Because I Said So

So Helen, from someone who's been there, done that and got the beamer, please try to laugh it all off.

Because, in the blink of an eye, you might be facing the most tortuous of my parenting episodes so far – the moment my sixteen-year-old decided to leave home and venture off to follow his sporting ambitions. We discussed it, I agreed, hugged him and told him it'll be great. And it will.

But the thought of letting him fly the nest already?

Pass the Jaffa Cakes because it doesn't get much worse than that. ◆

Anatomy of a Bump

I have a new favourite celebrity mum. Becky Vardy, wife of footballer, Jamie Vardy, got so sick of trolls calling her 'huge' after the birth of her son, Finley, that she posed for a gorgeous photo shoot in her undies, proudly showing off – in her words – her 'wobbly tummy, bigger legs, wrinkled skin and stretch marks'.

In other words, she looked normal. And beautiful. And happy.

I'd do a Mexican wave of solidarity, but after many years of breastfeeding, it's not a wise move without the support of a sports bra from the maximum-control section.

That's just life. Basic anatomy.

Alas, on Planet Celebrity, you'd never know it. Day after day we're confronted with images of stars who are back in their size-six Versace jeans within an hour and a half of popping out their little Gucci-booteed darling.

For some lucky women, the instant return of their former

figure is just one of nature's blessings. For far too many others, it's the result of intense diet and exercise plans, born of a need to look fabulous in a Snapchat story or *OK!* glossy spread.

Even the thought of it is exhausting. When God was giving out bungee-esque abdominals that could snap back into shape within a nanosecond of childbirth, I was behind the door, having tea and toast and committing the pain to memory so I'd have something to blackmail the kids with when they're older.

Incidentally, Low the Elder – that thirty-two-hour labour explains why I glaze over when you moan about being asked to spend ten minutes running round the house with a Dyson.

Back to the lumpy point.

Today's mass coverage of famous names in all their airbrushed or pampered perfection creates unrealistic expectations for the rest of womankind. And the comparisons don't just start when several pounds of human being has been delivered safely into the world.

I'm fascinated by Amal Clooney. She's stunning, brilliant, smart and very pregnant with twins. In every photograph, she is a paragon of calm, impeccably groomed serenity.

However, just in case any women out there are feeling even a tiny bit inadequate because they haven't donned an outfit from House of Chanel and spoken at the United Nations this week, I'd just like to redress the big bump balance.

According to fashionistas, Amal's pregnancy wardrobe

wouldn't leave enough change for a box of Pampers out of £170K. That's not a clothing collection, it's a semi-detached house.

When I was six months pregnant, I was the size of a garden shed, and ventured to House of Matalan for leggings, tunics, and knickers that could comfortably double as a cover for the patio set.

And that's why Becky's photo shoot is so important. In a world where it often seems that nothing matters more than the illusion of physical perfection, it's good for new mums to see that, in the reality show of life, some versions of motherhood come with snap-back abs. Some come with a wobble. And some come with a Mexican wave and maximum-control sports bra. ◆

And now... sob...

Empty Nest

Public Warning - these final words were written by an emotional mother, aided by a large dose of nostalgia and a box of Kleenex. Sniff.

I can still remember the very moment I found out I'd been offered a weekly newspaper column. The call came in during the week before Christmas 2003. Our boys were spending the day with their auntie, and husband and I were celebrating surviving the festive shopping scrum with a quick game of pool in a local bar. I blame excitement for the fact that I missed the next three shots.

My remit was simple: with two children under three, my job was to write about the funny, worrying, stressful, happy, bizarre, brilliant and quirky things that happened in our family every week.

Empty Nest

I've never had to look too far for material.

There was the big meeting with a Hollywood producer that was almost scuppered by a wee boy and a protest situation regarding Buzz Lightyear pull-up pants.

Then came the nursery days when I wrestled with all those work/stay at home, eat organic/commando-crawl into McDonalds, Tweenies/Teletubbies dilemmas.

I wrote about their first days at school, their nativity plays, and the summer holidays that involved baking buckets of cupcakes, a league of footie sessions, and a visit to a chiropractor when I put my back out while teaching Low the Elder to ride a bike.

My annual Christmas debacles made it on to the page every year. And, no, I still haven't managed to cook an entire yuletide feast without a seismic disaster – but, thankfully, my lovely extended clan still keeps coming back.

Our jollies to shores near and far usually had a similar theme of mayhem and bedlam. I may never recover from the staycation to a rain-soaked Loch Tay with four mums, seven sons and twenty-two wellies. And our brood are so injury-prone that we began to choose our holidays by locating a fabulous hospital and booking a fortnight all-inclusive at the nearest beach resort.

Today, daily life is a million miles away from that phone call almost fourteen years ago.

It's now the summer of 2017 and my boys are fifteen and sixteen. Low the Elder passed all his exams, got selected to play basketball for both Scotland and Great Britain and he is fleeing the nest this month, off to bounce a ball at a sports academy far from home. Low the Younger still belts out a tune on the saxophone, when he's not playing basketball for the Scotland U16 squad and conceding to my pathetic pleas to accompany me to the latest superhero flick. Chances are that if he manages to scale the barricades I've propped against the front door, he'll follow his brother on the road to independence in the not too distant future. Another sniff.

As soon as they started school, I stopped using my sons' names in this column, choosing to protect their privacy while they grew up.

Now they're shaving and in possession of their own front door keys, I'm lifting the ban for this final chapter.

Callan and Brad Low, thank you. You're still, and will always be, my favourite people on earth and I've adored every minute of being your mother – even the ones that involved eye-rolling and huffs. I'll miss doing that.

And as we start on the next chapter that will take you into fully fledged adulthood, I just want to ask that you abide by a couple of conditions.

Call me every day – and pretend that you don't mind, don't think I'm over-protective, and that I'm not listed as 'It's Her Again' in your phone contacts.

You must visit your parents at least once a week, otherwise I'll hunt you down.

Your first tattoo had better say 'I love Mum'.

Empty Nest

If I ever get another shot at that meeting with a Hollywood producer, please make sure you don't cause any underwear-related delays.

And if Dad and I go missing the first weekend after you've moved out?

We'll be in the pub, having the long-awaited rematch from that pool game in 2003...

Love you more than words. Because I said so.

Mum x ◆

Glossary

Bahookies	Bottoms. Buttocks. Gluteus Maximus. Arse. Level of profanity depending on circumstances.
Ball crawl	soft play area inhabited by over-excited children and frazzled parents who've learned to block out the noise for the pay off of a few snatched minutes of peace, a cup of tea and a Bakewell Tart.
Beamer	the red face caused by a mortifying situation. Also applies to the person causing the embarrassment. Or in our family's case, the noun most commonly used by my sons to describe their mother.
Burdz/burds	an alternative term for 'woman' – used in the days before political correctness, generally directed at myself and preceded by the word 'chunky'.

Dooking for apples	an ancient Halloween tradition involving removing apples from a barrel of water without using hands. Probably now barred due to some over-zealous Health and Safety legislation.
Napper	head.
Oxters	armpits.
A petted lip	the protruding bottom lip, often witnessed on a small child who is sad, scared, or in the huff because you've switched off CBeebies.
Plook	a facial spot.
A punty	the act of clasping hands in order to make a support from which to propel another human being upwards. Usually deployed when I can't find the ladders to retrieve the Christmas tree from the loft. Can occasionally result in the requirement for medical attention (apologies again to the husband for the Christmas 2007/ slipped disc trauma).
Pure gallus	bold, brave, fearless and displaying ample quantities of self-confidence.
Shoogled	deliberately shook. When referring to the buttock area, modern equivalent would be 'twerked' or 'doing a Miley'.
Sook	Scottish term for 'suck'.
A square go	a physical fight usually without weapons – the exception involving small children and household objects masquerading as light sabers.

Glossary

Stookie   the plaster applied to bone fractures, especially prevalent in the Junior Lows' pre-school superhero phases.

Acknowledgements

Many of these columns, or versions of them, were originally printed in the *Daily Record* newspaper.

My sincere thanks to Allan Rennie, Managing Director and Editor in Chief of Media Scotland, and the *Daily Record* editors past and present for letting me share my stories of family life.

Thanks too to the fantastic publishing team at Head Of Zeus, and especially to the three wonderful women who made this book happen. Caroline Ridding, for loving the original idea. Amanda Ridout for supporting the project from the start. And Ellen Parnavelas, who took it on board, made it happen and shaped it into the book it is today. I feel incredibly lucky to be part of the Head Of Zeus/Aria/ Anima family.

Endless gratitude to my sons, Callan and Brad, for allowing me to publish embarrassing tales of their childhood. Boys, please don't worry that I've spilled all of the excruciating ones… I've kept a couple of corkers for your 21st birthday parties and your wedding days.

And finally, thanks to everyone who has read my columns, features and novels over the years. I hope you love this book as much as I enjoyed writing every single story in it.

Love, Shari x